T0088018

BALTIMORE ORIOLES
WHERE HAVE YOU GONE?

CAL RIPKEN JR., BROOKS ROBINSON, JIM PALMER, AND OTHER ORIOLES GREATS

JEFF SEIDEL

SPORTS
PUBLISHING

All photos courtesy of Stuart Zolotorow/Studio Z Photography, unless otherwise noted.

Sports Publishing books may be purchased in bulk at special discounts for sales promotion, corporate gifts, fund-raising, or educational purposes. Special editions can also be created to specifications. For details, contact the Special Sales Department, Sports Publishing, 307 West 36th Street, 11th Floor, New York, NY 10018 or sportspubbooks@skyhorsepublishing.com.

Sports Publishing® is a registered trademark of Skyhorse Publishing, Inc.®, a Delaware corporation.

Visit our website at www.sportspubbooks.com.

10 9 8 7 6 5 4 3 2 1

Library of Congress Cataloging-in-Publication Data is available on file.

ISBN: 978-1-61321-634-7

Printed in the United States of America

For my *home team. Nadine, Zach, and Kara.*
You're still all winners.

And for Alan Bieler, the very definition of the word "friend."
We miss you.

CONTENTS

ACKNOWLEDGMENTS

T his is an update of the book that I wrote nine years ago. We've added some new information to it, updating some old things and giving it a bit of a different look. First, my thanks to folks at Skyhorse Publishing for wanting to do this update. Julie Ganz guided me on this, answered my endless e-mails, and brought the project to the finish line. It was a pleasure to work with her.

Baseball has been a big part of my life since the age of seven. I've learned that it's like life; you've just got to keep on pushing and trying. One person who taught me that lesson was my good friend Alan Bieler. A huge Red Sox fan, he always knew how to do keep battling, spending the last three years of his life in that mode when it came to cancer treatments. I never saw anyone so tough or determined. He lost that battle about a year ago, but his lessons will never be forgotten.

He also was the godfather to my daughter, Kara. She battles through various things also and keeps on going in a way that makes me shake my head every day. This skinny 17-year old has the toughness of an NFL line-backer. Thanks to Kara and my wife, Nadine, and son, Zach, for still dealing with me. They both are tough cookies, too. Don't get in their way. Trust me on that one.

Thanks also to Neil Rubin, the biggest baseball freak I knew as a kid. Sorry, now it's Dr. Rubin. I'm having a hard time with that one. And thanks to Ari Rubin, one of the smartest teenagers I've ever met when it comes to baseball. He really knows his stuff, and they both helped me with this update. My good friend, Todd Karpovich, is a pleasure to work with and one of the best sounding boards any person could have.

My two nephews, Matthew and Jeremy Enslin, live in New Jersey and aren't Oriole fans, but we can only do so much. Now, my nephew who lives in Baltimore, Maxwell Jolbitado, is a big Oriole fan. He'll like reading this more. My nieces, Lily and Jenna Handwerger, also fall into that category. Or so I hope.

Thanks also to my mom, Elaine Seidel (never a baseball fan, but that's life), and my in-laws, Muriel and Leroy Handwerger for all of their kindness and support. It's very much appreciated.

Editor's Note:

This book was originally published in 2006. Though we've worked to bring the book up to date, most of the information and player quotes come from the 2006 text.

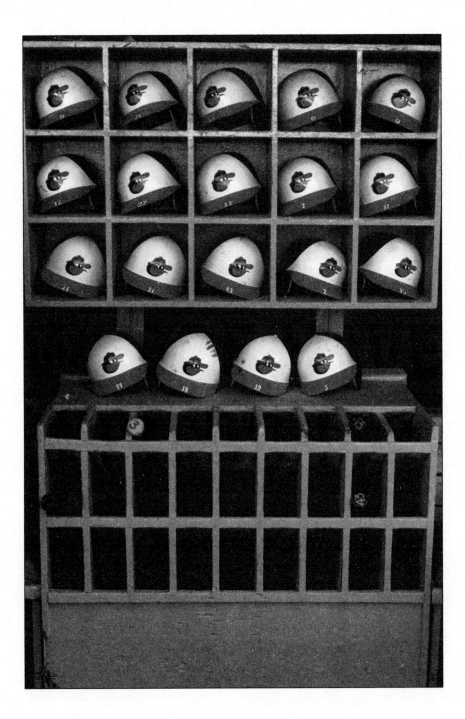

Where Have You Gone?

ERNIE TYLER

The Man Who Made Cal's Streak Look Small

E rnie Tyler was a baseball oxymoron. He's the man who everybody who
follows Orioles baseball recognizes but nobody knew.

Orioles fans witnessed Tyler sitting on his stool by the dugout for years.
They know that he's the guy who ran out and handed the home plate umpire baseballs when the need would arise—yet nobody realized exactly what
he did, and many didn't know exactly who he was.

Or how very long he'd done it.

Tyler started his job as the umpire's attendant during the 1960 season when the Orioles played at old Memorial Stadium and hasn't missed
a game since. At the end of the 2005 season, that meant that Tyler had
worked 3,686 consecutive games, a number that far passed Cal Ripken
Jr.'s famous streak and helped Tyler gain induction into the team's Hall of
Fame during the 2004 season.

Changes in Oriole Park and Camden Yards moved Tyler from a stool
by the third-base dugout to stand next to the home team's dugout on the
first base side. In 2004, Baltimore honored him with the Herb Armstrong
Award, given to non-uniformed personnel who've made a significant contribution to the ball club, community, or sport of baseball.

Many people came out on the day that Tyler got the award in 2004—
big-name people—to pay tribute to the man who'd been helping them
around the clubhouse and the man they'd seen for, well, a few decades.

"It's a tremendous honor," Tyler said. "It doesn't really fit until right
now. I just think it's a super honor."

And what did Tyler do in the minutes before getting the honor? The
same thing as always—he worked. Standing in the hallway that leads to the

Jerry Wachter/Baltimore Orioles

ERNIE TYLER • UMPIRES ATTENDANT

Best Season with the Orioles: All of them
Highlights: Tyler put together a Cal Ripken Jr.-like streak, having compiled 3,819 consecutive games for the Orioles. He's the guy you saw running out to hand the umpires baseballs—and also was there way before the game to help the men in blue get everything they need to call the game.

tunnel behind home plate where the umpires and anyone else can go, Tyler treated the day he made his mark in Orioles history the same as any other. He kept going in and out of the umpires' room to make sure the men in blue had all that they needed to work that day's game.

Meanwhile, Tyler's large family celebrated in a room just a few feet away. Sitting with famous Orioles such as Jim Palmer, Cal Ripken, Earl Weaver, and others, the 43 members of the Tyler brigade relaxed. They sat in what serves as the stadium's auxiliary clubhouse to have a dinner before that day's late afternoon game. Tyler and his wife, Juliane, had 11 children, and there were many Tylers talking with the man of honor while he worked.

Palmer and others complimented Tyler before, during, and after the ceremony that day.

"It's great to see that smiling face," Palmer said. "He has so many friends."

But everyone with the Orioles family often compared him to Ripken for several reasons. Both had connections to Harford County, which is north of Baltimore. Ripken is from there, and Tyler lived in the county.

And everyone knows about Ripken's streak. But Tyler's isn't bad, either, something that Ripken paid tribute to during the season.

"We ... know who the true Iron Man is in Baltimore, Ernie Tyler," said Ripken, whose record streak of playing in 2,632 games probably won't ever be passed.

Much like Ripken, Tyler made his mark with very hard work. The best-known parts of Tyler's job were the bringing of baseballs to the umpires and the way he sat and rubbed mud on the balls before the game to get them ready for play. He'd often seat himself in the umpire's room at Oriole Park under the stands and actually not very far from home plate to cover the balls with a layer of mud.

Tyler also did whatever the umpires needed to help get them ready for the game. It's a thankless but necessary job—and one Tyler's did for more than four decades. And it's something that he loved to do.

He started out with the team doing part-time work, and Tyler eventually got a shot at the job full-time. It was supposed to be on a trial basis at the start of the 1960 season, and Tyler simply kept going.

"I guess I've still got it," Tyler said with a laugh during the 2004 season.

Tyler was a graduate of Baltimore's Mount St. Joseph School, a private school on the edge of the city that's now very well known for its strong boys' basketball, wrestling, football, and hockey teams. While at St. Joe, he played on the same football team as Frank Cashen, later a general manager with the Orioles and then the Mets.

He joined the Orioles as a part-time usher when the team returned to Baltimore in 1954. Tyler became a full-time usher four years later before going to his current position for the 1960 season. All of this was made even more impressive by the fact that Tyler worked a full-time job with state's Department of Health and Mental Hygiene for many years before retiring in 1988.

Being the father of 11 kids also took some time. But Tyler moved some of his family to the ballgames as nine members of his family—including Ernie and his wife—worked for the Orioles at some point. In fact, Jim and Fred Tyler were still working as the home and visiting team clubhouse managers while their dad tended to the umpires.

Ernie Tyler rarely liked to be in the spotlight or around it. That explains why he didn't spend much time celebrating with his family on the day of his big honor with the Orioles. He clearly felt uncomfortable with the attention on him. But that's what low-key personalities are like.

Tyler never changed from when he started his job in 1960. He simply focused on doing what he did as best he can.

"I just enjoy what I do," Tyler said.

Tyler battled some health problems before he passed away in 2011 at the age of 86. He worked in 3,819 consecutive games in Baltimore with the umpires before the streak ended in late July of 2007, upon which time he went to Ripken's Hall of Fame induction.

BILL RIPKEN

Keeping It in the Family

S ome people get jealous or feel overshadowed by an older brother who's tremendously successful in the same field. However, Bill Ripken is certainly not one of those people.

Not only did he appreciate what his older brother, Cal Jr., could do in baseball, but Bill felt grateful to have played with him for a long period of time. In addition, Bill strongly followed the philosophies his father (Cal Sr.) taught. Simply put, learning from his father and playing with a Hall of Fame-style brother helped Bill throughout his career.

It's also something that's been a big part of his life after Bill's major league career ended in 1998. He's been working with Cal Jr. to help run the Aberdeen (Maryland) IronBirds minor league team and is the co-owner of the Ripken Baseball company with his brother. The mission of that company is to spread baseball and the teaching of it "The Ripken Way." Cal and Bill worked tirelessly to teach baseball everywhere to children, emphasizing things like fundamentals and playing as a team, something that some younger kids are having a harder time understanding during a time when being self-centered has become the rule rather than the exception.

"The do-it-right philosophy we have is still there," Bill Ripken said. "When we went out there to play, we had a job to do. That was my dad's philosophy. You don't half-ass it. You do it to be done right, and that's what I think we [do] best."

Bill has worked a lot with kids trying to stress the importance of their enjoying baseball as much as learning it. Ripken Baseball has been doing a tournament similar to the Little League World Series, bringing teams in from all over the country and the world—the 2004 competition had groups

Bill Ripken 2B
ORIOLES

#3 BILL RIPKEN • 2B
Seasons with the Orioles: 1987-1992, 1996

Best Season with the Orioles: 1990
Highlight Stats from that Season: Ripken had his best offensive year that season. Even though he hit .308 in 58 games in 1987, this was Ripken's best full season. He hit a career-best .291 with three homers and 38 RBI along with a career-high 118 hits in 126 games.

from places like Mexico, Korea, and Connecticut—while Cal and Bill were all over Ripken Stadium talking with children, signing autographs, and just chatting.

"We [have] the same standard of [doing things right] now," Bill said. "We don't worry too much about what other people do. We worry about tending to our own shop."

The IronBirds have been a huge success from day one. The team plays in a new stadium about 30 miles north of Oriole Park at Camden Yards—both are right off exits on I-95—and sold out every home game in their shorter season for the first four years. They quickly gained a huge following in Aberdeen despite the fact that minor league ball gives each city mostly different rosters each season.

But the IronBirds, despite their quick success, are just part of what the Ripkens do. They work with camps and clinics, getting their baseball message out to the world the way they want it.

"I think that, as far as Ripken Baseball goes, we're starting to surround ourselves with what we feel are pretty smart people," Bill said. "You bring in people to do what they do, but you certainly don't go away and won't be used. Between me and Cal, we're not short on ideas, and these people help us make it happen."

Bill Ripken had to make things happen his own way during his baseball career. Coming to the Orioles in 1987, he combined with older brother Cal Jr., to form one of baseball's best double-play combinations for the next several seasons.

Staying with the Orioles through 1992, Ripken later played for Texas, Cleveland, and Detroit and also had another stint with Baltimore as a utility player in 1996. That's when the Orioles gave the New York Yankees a fight for the American League East championship but came up a little short before making the playoffs as the wild card.

When asked about what his most memorable moment in the majors was, Ripken paused for a moment and said picking one would be tough.

"Probably looking back, you didn't know what you had till it was gone," he said. "But the mere fact that I played alongside Cal as long as I did, and the fact that my first big league manager was my dad and Cal was at short... Dad managed two sons on the big league on the same team, and that was the first time in history it happened. I'm very, very proud of that."

The Orioles were struggling at that time. Baltimore had been one of baseball's top teams from the mid-1960s through the mid-1980s, but fell after winning the World Series in 1983. They had another winning season in 1984 but had to watch from far behind as Detroit jumped to a 35-5 start, ran away with the East, and later won the World Series.

But everything started to fall apart after that. Ripken's father took over as manager in 1987 after Earl Weaver ended his comeback attempt. Ripken was left with a team filled with veteran stars who had seen better days. The Orioles finished 67-95 and 31 games out of first in the East, and when the team lost its first six games of 1988, the club made a move that surprised some by firing Ripken after an April 12 loss and replacing him with former star Frank Robinson. It didn't help much as the Orioles went on to lose their major league-record 21 straight games to open the season.

But the move clearly stung both Bill and Cal Jr. Bill showed his support for his father by changing his number from 3 to 7—what Cal Sr. was wearing—as a tribute to his dad.

"Obviously, I was hurt by the whole thing," Bill said. "I just looked at Dad as being No. 7. I really didn't want anything going on during the course of the year, and it just occurred to me that somebody else could be given No. 7, and I just didn't like that thought very much. I just couldn't bear to think about it at that time."

Bill Ripken had a tougher time than his older brother. He was always the one who had to show his abilities every year. There wasn't always a guaranteed roster spot awaiting him when he went to spring training in Florida. So what did he have to do? Let the Orioles see how good he was—and Bill Ripken understood that.

"There were times when I went to spring training as a non-roster player and was 28th or 29th on the depth chart," he said. "But I felt strongly that if I went there and showed what I could do, I'd come out on the top 25 and on the roster."

That's usually what happened. During his time with the Orioles, Ripken proved to be a solid defensive player like his brother and a pretty good hitter, although fielding was his strong point. Over 12 seasons, Ripken made only 61 errors. He had 674 hits and ended up with major league memories that were good ones, since the majority of his career was spent playing alongside his brother. Bill Ripken loved baseball when playing it and still is enraptured by the game now, several years after his playing career ended.

That's one reason he enjoyed playing next to his brother. Simply put, he appreciated everything that Cal Jr. did.

"He did things physically at shortstop that would wow me once a week," Bill said. "I don't think that people gave him enough credit. He was big,

Bill Ripken, Mike Bordick, Cal Ripken Jr., Doug DeCinces, and Brooks Robinson

and he was long, but he did have range. To lead the league in total putouts and total chances, you can't be a desert cactus."

Ripken's now works as a studio analyst for MLB Tonight and MLB Network's studio programs. He was nominated for a Sports Emmy Award for Outstanding Sports Personality in 2012.

JIM GENTILE

Diamond Jim

T he Baltimore Orioles had a number of big-time sluggers during
their history—Boog Powell, Frank Robinson, Eddie Murray, Rafael
Palmeiro, and others. But Jim Gentile was the first and most well known.

Gentile anchored the lineup when the Orioles began to find success
in 1960 and had a spectacular season in 1961. And even though the team
traded him a few years later, Baltimore fans still remembered him when
voting for the team's 50th anniversary club in 2004. It was something Gentile couldn't believe—and he was thrilled to get a chance to return to Baltimore for a celebration.

Gentile has done many things since retiring in the mid-1960s. Living
in Oklahoma, Gentile had gone down a number of different paths with
his life—both in and out of baseball. The man they called "Diamond Jim"
owned a Midas franchise, managed a department store, and retired from
the business world at the age of 57. But he also kept his hand in baseball,
managing in some independent leagues, because he had a hard time staying
away from the game he loved so much.

"I really enjoy doing that," Gentile said.

Gentile did several things to help Orioles fans remember him during
his four years with the team, most of which came during a memorable
1961 season. The Orioles had finally broken through in the baseball world
in 1960, challenging the mighty New York Yankees all the way into September before fading and finishing in second place with a team filled with
young prospects and players who would eventually be very good. Baltimore
didn't challenge quite as much in 1961, despite having many of the same
players back and winning 95 games.

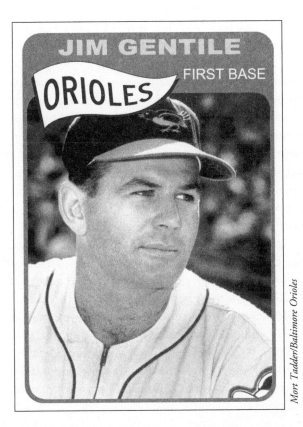

JIM GENTILE

FIRST BASE

ORIOLES

Mort Tadder/Baltimore Orioles

#4 JIM GENTILE • 1B
Seasons with the Orioles: 1960-1963

Best Season with the Orioles: 1961
Highlight Stats from that Season: Gentile had a tremendous year, hitting 46 homers and driving in 141 runs with a .302 average. He made the All-Star Game and finished among the American League leaders in numerous categories—but his accomplishments might have been overshadowed a bit by the famous home-run race between Roger Maris and Mickey Mantle.

The Orioles finished third that year, 14 games out, while the Yankees won the pennant once more. But that was Gentile's year in Baltimore. He kind of got caught in the long shadow cast by Roger Maris that season when the Yankees outfielder broke Babe Ruth's record with 61 homers. But plenty of people noticed, as the first baseman had the best year of his career, pounding out 46 home runs with 141 RBI. Gentile also set a new American League record with five grand slams that season.

But Gentile's biggest moment came on May 9 when he became the third player in history to hit grand slams in consecutive innings as the Orioles scored a 13-5 rout of the expansion Twins. Gentile started things by blasting a grand slam off Pedro Ramos in the first inning and followed it with another slam off Paul Giel in the second.

Gentile later added a sacrifice fly to finish with a club-record nine RBI. Gentile finished with the aforementioned five grand slams—the fifth coming in Baltimore's 8-6 victory over Chicago on September 22. He also finished the season by hitting homers with 46 men on base, the most since Babe Ruth homered with 48 runners on base 40 years earlier.

At season's end, Gentile finished third in the American League Most Valuable Player voting, behind Roger Maris and Mickey Mantle. Maris edged Mantle by only four votes that year despite setting a new major league record with 61 homers. Gentile said playing on a good young team was a big reason that he got so many RBI—there were always men on base for him.

"We started with the Kiddie Korps in 1960 (the nickname for the young players on the team that year) and just went on from there," Gentile said. "We had a good team."

Gentile had begun his career in New York, playing in the Brooklyn Dodgers' farm system. Roy Campanella hung the nickname "Diamond Jim" on Gentile, and the moniker stuck throughout his career. The Dodgers traded him to Baltimore in 1960, however, a move that proved good for both Gentile and the Orioles.

Gentile made the All-Star team in his rookie year, hitting .292 with 21 homers. He also finished third in the Rookie of the Year voting. Gentile made the All-Star team again in 1961 during his career year and followed it up with a third straight appearance in 1962 after blasting 33 homers.

But Gentile said he knew his days in Baltimore were coming to an end despite his great success. The Orioles had a first baseman in the minors they were high on, and Gentile said he knew that when Boog Powell would be ready, the job would go to him. Powell was the kind of player teams get excited about, and the big first baseman would come on to hit 339 major

league homers, most of which came with the Orioles, and in the pre-designated hitter days, there was room for only one starting first baseman.

The Orioles traded Gentile to the Kansas City A's in 1964. He hit 28 homers that year, but never did that well again. Kansas City traded him to Houston during the 1965 season, and the Astros later traded Gentile to Cleveland. Gentile then retired about a year and a half later after a stint in Japan.

Gentile found some bad luck in Japan. He went to the Far East hoping for good luck, but everything went wrong from the start.

"I was thinking that I was going to like it," Gentile said. "But on Opening Day, I ruptured my Achilles tendon. They couldn't release me, because I had a guaranteed contract, so I sat and watched sumo wrestling for three months."

He said it was tough leaving the Orioles, because he could see how the young team was starting to come together as a winner. Gentile knew how good the pitchers were; he certainly saw how Brooks Robinson was beginning to develop into a big-time third baseman—he was named the

American League's MVP in 1964—and thought there were big times ahead for the team.

However, he also could read the cards and see what might be happening with his future.

"I hated to leave," Gentile said. "But it was just a question of [Orioles manager Hank] Bauer wanting his roommate from the Yankees, and they got rid of me. And you knew Boog was going to play first base; it was just a matter of when. I hated to leave. Believe me, I wanted to finish my career here."

Jim Gentile was one of the older players the Orioles honored at their 50th anniversary celebration in 2004. When asked how it felt to be back in Baltimore, the easy-going former slugger simply laughed.

"It's unbelievable," he said. "I didn't think there were that many people living that still remembered us."

As Gentile was talking in one of the clubhouses at Oriole Park at Camden Yards, Powell stood several feet away, and the two men talked. There was no bitterness as each admired the other. They talked and laughed for several minutes as they swapped stories about baseball and life. Gentile couldn't stop smiling. He was thrilled to be remembered more than 40 years after his greatest days and just loved being in a major league ballpark once more.

"I feel good, and I'm very lucky," Gentile said. "Everybody's been really nice to me, and it's great to be back in Baltimore again."

Gentile, though retired, made some baseball news in 2010 when he got a $5,000 bonus from the Orioles. The team had said they'd give him that money if he led the American League in RBI in 1961, but Gentile finished second with 141, just behind Roger Maris (142). However, the New York Times reported in the summer of 2010 that the Elias Sports Bureau officially recognized an RBI change that brought Maris back to 141. And so the Orioles presented Gentile with a $5,000 check before a game.

BROOKS ROBINSON

A Baltimore Legend

M inor league baseball is growing in popularity in the mid-Atlantic area. The Bowie Baysox and Frederick Keys are Baltimore Orioles affiliates, and each has been entrenched in their communities for many years. That's one reason that more minor league teams are starting to come to the area.

Minor league teams in nearby York and Lancaster, a pair of Pennsylvania towns within 90 minutes of Oriole Park, were being put together in the winter of 2005 under the hand of Peter Kirk, who helped start both the Bowie and Frederick franchises several years ago. Kirk's company also was looking to start another team down in Charles County in Southern Maryland and brought in one of the best names in Baltimore baseball history to help out.

Hall of Famer Brooks Robinson has helped out with the minor league franchises in a number of ways. He's been involved with a number of decisions on and off the field, trying to make the Lancaster Barnstormers, the York franchise, and the Southern Maryland Blue Crabs into strong teams. Robinson hasn't been involved with baseball on the field since retiring late in the 1977 season. He had his chances, turning away opportunities to look at managing the Chicago White Sox and the Texas Rangers, but now he gets to work in a different capacity.

"It's been fun for me," Robinson said. "I follow the game still. I watch games on TV, and I don't go to many of them. Helping run the new minor league teams in Lancaster and York... helping pick players and coaches, that's going to be the fun part of it."

#5 BROOKS ROBINSON • 3B
Seasons with the Orioles: 1955-1977

Best Season with the Orioles: 1964
Highlight Stats from that Season: Robinson won the American League
Most Valuable Player award that year in a break-out season. He finished
with 28 homers, 118 RBI, and a .317 average—all career bests. The Hall
of Famer also finished second in the league in average and first in RBI,
and became a power hitter to be reckoned with for the
next several seasons.

Robinson is probably the best-known name in Baltimore baseball history for fans 45 and older—just like Cal Ripken Jr. holds that place for younger fans. Many older Baltimore fans and media members often said that Ripken was their generation's Brooks Robinson.

Robinson was loved in Baltimore for many of the same reasons as Ripken. He grew into an iron man who missed few games and made even fewer mistakes in the field. Ripken would stay late after games to sit and give kids autographs for long amounts of time—when there were no cameras around. He did it for his love of the game and the children. Robinson was a similar personality. The Arkansas native's Southern charm, bright smile, and easy demeanor won people over instantly. He made you feel like a friend even after meeting him for the first time. There just was a way about him.

But Robinson was different from well-known players in other ways—starting with the fact that he truly walked away from the game when his playing career ended. In fact, Robinson agreed to stop playing with a little over a month left in a 1977 season when he barely saw time on the field to let the Orioles make a roster move that would help them in a battle for first place with the Red Sox and eventual world champion Yankees. That was a very unselfish move that likely wouldn't happen in the me-first generation of today.

He turned down the aforementioned managerial chances and became a color commentator on the Orioles television broadcasts for 16 years. Robinson stopped that in the early 1990s and stayed in private business before starting to help again with the minor league teams.

"I had several chances to manage in the major leagues since I left the game back in 1977," Robinson said. "I [then] talked to the White Sox and Texas about managing, and I really wasn't interested. The next year, the television job came open, and I started doing that. I had a good run there, 16 years, and my last child got married in 1993, so it was just time to slow down."

He also was loved for a more basic reason by the Baltimore baseball fans. He came through in the clutch. Over and over and over again, when the Baltimore Orioles needed a hit, Brooks Robinson found a way to come up with it. For example, the Orioles were the surprise team of 1966, making the World Series for the first time, and guess what Robinson did on his first at-bat? He blasted a homer that, along with teammate Frank Robinson's homer, gave the Orioles a jump-start to a 5-2 win that day. Baltimore went on to sweep the shocked Los Angeles Dodgers in four games. When Robinson hit his 200th career homer during the 1970 season, it wound up being a three-run shot that gave the Orioles a win.

But it was what happened at the end of the 1970 season that proved so crucial to Robinson's career. The Orioles made the World Series for the second straight year and had a bit of a chip on their shoulders after having lost to the surprising New York Mets in five games the year before. Robinson was one of the Orioles who never got going at the plate, ending up just one for 19 when the strong New York pitching staff shut down the tough Baltimore batters. However, everything changed in 1970 when the Orioles beat the Cincinnati Reds in five games with Robinson pulling off one of the most complete performances seen in any World Series.

Robinson made spectacular defensive plays throughout the Series. The best-known play came in Game 1. That's when Cincinnati first baseman Lee May hit a rocket over the third base bag, which Robinson backhanded in foul ground. He then spun and fired a strike that bounced right to first baseman Boog Powell, nailing May by a step. The play became famous instantly—and has been replayed thousands of times since. Robinson helped out again later by hitting the tie-breaking solo homer that gave Baltimore a crucial 4-3 victory. He made a diving catch of a Johnny Bench line drive in Game 3 and a similar diving play in Game 5. Robinson had four hits in Game 4, but Cincinnati rallied for a 6-5 win to stay alive. The Orioles clinched the championship the next day. Robinson finished the World Series with a .429 batting average and earned the Series' Most Valuable Player honor.

"You know, 1970 was a strange Series because we lost to the Mets in '69, and I think I got one hit in that Series—so you never know what's going to happen," Robinson said. "But in that particular Series, every game I had a chance to do something outstanding defensively. I was hitting well, too."

Robinson jokingly remembers feeling some pressure during the Series because of all of the plays that kept happening.

"I can remember after the third game, I'm saying, 'Man, I hope this gets over in a hurry,'" Robinson said with a laugh. "'I can't keep this up.' The story I always [tell] people is when the Series was over, they interviewed my glove instead of me."

Robinson still shakes his head when talking about that Series and how everything went right for him over a six-day period that he'll never forget.

"I played almost 23 years, and I don't think I ever had five games in a row like that, defensively and offensively," Robinson said. "And that was a five-game series that just happened to be in the World Series."

Mike Cuellar and Brooks Robinson

Robinson also said there's no doubt in his mind that the success he found against the Reds played a large role in his being voted into the Hall of Fame during the summer of 1983.

The big reason is that it put Robinson onto a bigger and brighter stage for a longer period of time. Robinson already was well known, having won the American League's Most Valuable Player award in 1964 after hitting .317 with 28 homers and 118 RBI. He also captured the All-Star Game MVP honor two years later.

But doing what he did against Cincinnati made him even more well known across the national baseball stage.

"That was certainly a springboard for me attaining the Hall of Fame, that part of it," Robinson said. "Getting into the World Series, getting the recognition, I think that's part of it. You know, there's a lot of guys that I've talked to, like Ernie Banks and George Kell, whom I went into the Hall of Fame with, and the one thing they seemed to miss in their careers is they never got a chance to play in the World Series. But that certainly helped me attain the Hall of Fame."

However, despite having such a memorable World Series in 1970 and playing in it four times overall, Robinson said that the Orioles' surprise sweep of the Dodgers in 1966 really ranks as the moment that is top on his list.

"I can remember saying, after it was all said and done, that hey, if you never win again, that was your dream—to be the world's champion," Robinson said. "Fortunately, we got to do it one more time... but that was still my favorite moment."

Robinson had some spectacular moments in the big games. He batted .348 in five American League Championship Series, .263 in the four World Series, and .289 in 18 All-Star Games. Overall, he batted .303 with five homers and 22 RBI in 39 postseason games. He also batted .267 with 268 homers in 2,896 games. Robinson also did well in the field, winning 16 Gold Gloves at third base—consecutively, from 1960 to 1975.

Robinson's been battling health issues more in recent years, but he's also been recently recognized by the Orioles. Robinson was one of the former players who had a sculpture unveiled at the ballpark during 2012—and the fans' behavior that day showed how popular Robinson remained, 35 years after his retirement.

Where Have You Gone?

ANDY ETCHEBARREN

Just an Old-School Guy

A ndy Etchebarren got a new job for the 2005 season. He was headed back to the dugout to manage the Class A Aberdeen IronBirds. Some might look at that as heading downhill after having managed at Class AA and AAA, and coached and played in the majors. In fact, Etchebarren hadn't managed in a few years, but he is a person who loves being in the dugout and on the field—as a part of the game.

Etchebarren and baseball have been together for most of the time since signing to play with the Orioles after graduating high school in 1961. He just can't get the game out of his blood. He went on to play 12 full seasons in the majors and parts of three more—most of it with Baltimore. Etchebarren made the All-Star Game in his rookie year of 1966, and played a big role in helping Baltimore win its first American League title and then the World Series in a shocking four-game upset over Los Angeles.

Now more than 30 years after retiring, Etchebarren's face still lights up when talking about the sport.

"I love the game. There's no doubt that I love the game," Etchebarren said. "I like the players. The players have changed a little bit, but it's still baseball."

And if it's still baseball, then Etchebarren still loves it. He guided the IronBirds to a 27-48 record and did a great job working with the younger players the Orioles sent to the team owned by Cal Ripken Jr.

Etchebarren is a bit unusual. He's old school through and through. He comes from a time when players weren't so concerned if it was a contract year. They just played hard all the time and let everything take care of itself.

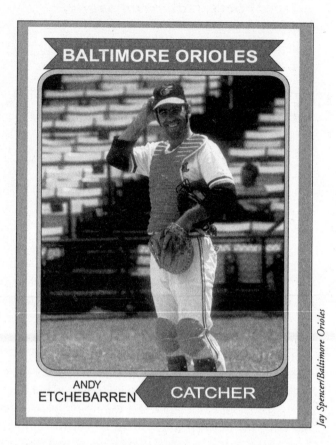

BALTIMORE ORIOLES

ANDY
ETCHEBARREN   CATCHER

Jay Spencer/Baltimore Orioles

#8 ANDY ETCHEBARREN • C
Seasons with the Orioles: 1962, 1965-1975

Best Season with the Orioles: 1966
Highlight Stats from that Season: He had a big season when serving as
the O's main catcher as a rookie in 1966. Etchebarren had career highs
in homers (11) and RBI (50), and made the All-Star Game despite hitting
just .221. He played a big part in the Orioles' winning the pennant and
then sweeping the Dodgers in the World Series.

He wants the players he works with to stick to that same formula—something that's tough at times in the me-first generation.

He clashed at times with players like Matt Riley, once considered to be a top pitching prospect with Baltimore, when the two were together at the team's Class AA Bowie farm site. Riley had a bit of an attitude—although not on purpose—he just liked to do things his way. When pitching under Etchebarren in 2000, the left-hander infuriated the skipper by trying to take shortcuts through different workout routines.

Etchebarren was livid with how Riley would be the last player to show up and then not want to do all of the running the club wanted. When Riley struggled for a while in the first part of the season, Etchebarren seethed. He finally called Riley in and laid down the law. Riley changed his act completely, and Etchebarren was very proud of how the left-hander turned things around in such a very short time.

"They have to work; you just can't get better and you can't reach your potential without hard work," Etchebarren said. "I really believe that. The thing that bothers me most when managing is that I could tell by looking at a pitcher and looking at a position player if I thought they had a pretty good chance to play in the big leagues. If they had good tools, it was my job to get them ready to play in the big leagues."

Etchebarren was ready to play in the big leagues from the start. Even though he hit only .221 in his rookie year (1966), it wound up being a career best for him in many ways. He had career bests in homers (11), RBI (50), games (121), runs (49), and hits (91). Everything went right for the Orioles that year en route to the championship, and even though he made it to the playoffs five more times with the Birds, that remains his favorite memory.

"The 1966 World Series is the top thing only because we had so many rookies on that team, and they didn't really give us much of a chance when the year started," Etchebarren said. "We went up the middle with three rookies, not counting pitchers, just myself behind the plate, Davey Johnson at second base, Paul Blair in center field, and they said you can't play with three rookies up the middle. But we all had decent years."

Etchebarren eventually split the starting catching role with Elrod Hendricks starting in 1969. It was a perfect match. Etchebarren was a right-hander, who was solid defensively but not as good at the plate. Hendricks was a left-handed hitter with plenty of power that he put on display many times.

But even though Etchebarren also struggled at times in postseason play, he came up big in his final playoff series. He went five for 14 in the 1974

American League Championship Series, which Oakland rallied to win three games to two.

Etchebarren's biggest hit came in Game 4 in Oakland, when the A's appeared ready to wrap up the series in four games. His three-run homer in the seventh inning sparked a four-run Orioles rally that tied the game. Second baseman Bobby Grich's solo shot in the eighth gave the Orioles the 5-4 win that forced Game 5.

Etchebarren also was well known for being able to handle the Orioles pitching staff well. He grew especially close to crafty left-hander Dave Mc-Nally. The two did a lot of good things together, starting with their first game as a Baltimore battery.

"Our first game in the major leagues was in 1962," Etchebarren said. "He came up from [the minor leagues], and he pitched a 2-0 shutout in just one hour and 32 minutes. It's still the shortest game in Baltimore history."

Playing for five playoff teams and two World Series winners was a big reason that Etchebarren always remained popular with Baltimore fans. He was picked as one of the 50 most popular players of the team's first 50 years in Baltimore, something that meant a lot to him.

"It's an honor, 50 years. If there's 50 guys, that's really one guy a year for 50 years," Etchebarren said. "That's pretty good to be a part of this group. I feel very fortunate, and I'm very happy to be a part of it."

Etchebarren managed the York Revolution of the Atlantic League from August, 2009, until stepping down and retiring after 2012. He coached in the major leagues, managed in the minors, and wound up being very successful at York.

Where Have You Gone?

CAL RIPKEN JR.

Cal: No Other Words Are Needed

M any baseball fans will remember Cal Ripken Jr. for breaking the one record everyone thought couldn't be touched. Lou Gehrig's mark of having played in 2,130 consecutive games just seemed impossible with the 162-game season, crazy scheduling, and travel that could wear down even the player in the greatest of shape.

But Ripken became known in Baltimore for much more than just that—and his reputation actually has grown after he retired following the 2001 season. He basically did what his father (Cal Ripken Sr.) did—he made baseball his life in different ways. And Ripken accomplished that in a way that certainly would have made his father proud. He simply went back to his old hometown, brought baseball there, and taught everyone about IronBirds.

Most baseball fans knew Ripken's numbers when he retired. He played with the Orioles for parts of 21 seasons. The great prospect, when coming to the team at the age of 20 late in 1981, broke new ground when then-manager Earl Weaver moved him from third base to shortstop a few weeks into his first year. A six-foot-four shortstop? In the major leagues? That just wasn't done. Shortstops were supposed to be small and quick enough to have the range so desperately needed for the position—but Weaver thought Ripken could do it.

And the skipper was right. Ripken knew how to cut corners, his ability to move an extra step here or there to help him get in a better position became legendary. When former Oriole Davey Johnson moved him back to third base, Ripken clearly thought he could still be a shortstop, but went to his new position and did his job well.

26

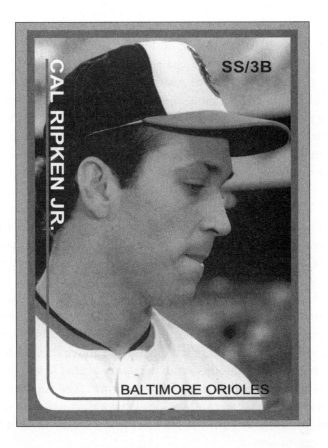

SS/3B

CAL RIPKEN JR.

BALTIMORE ORIOLES

#8 CAL RIPKEN JR. • SS/3B
Seasons with the Orioles: 1981-2001

Best Season with the Orioles: 1991
Highlight Stats from that Season: Ripken had a number of big seasons,
but this was probably his best. He had struggled for a few years and
bounced back in a big way, hitting a career-best .323 along with career
bests in homers (34) and RBI (114). Ripken also won the American
League Most Valuable Player honor and the All-Star Game MVP along
with his first Gold Glove at shortstop.

But Ripken took on a different role after his retirement. He kept baseball a huge part of his life. He and his brother, Bill, another former Oriole, started Ripken Baseball and purchased a minor league baseball team and moved it to their hometown of Aberdeen. They renamed them the Iron-Birds and built Ripken Stadium, and the town fell in love with everything. Trying to get an IronBirds ticket for their short season—June through August—can be a nearly impossible task because the team sells out constantly. Ripken Stadium looks more like a major league stadium than a minor league park, and the star is often there.

They also host the Ripken World Series there each August. A kind of a parallel to the Little League World Series, this tournament also brings in teams from all over the world. They stay in and around Aberdeen for several days and get a number of chances to meet Ripken and his brother. That's something unusual in this day of having to pay for autographs and players even asking for money to do interviews.

One thing that showed something about Ripken happened during his 2004 tournament. He had been at the stadium for a while during the day, and the games had ended around 9:30 p.m. By the time the teams from the last game had come out of their dugout and gotten dressed, it was after 10 p.m. But he and his brother sat in the stands behind home plate talking and chatting with the children—for a long time. The Ripkens answered questions about everything, and the kids left with big smiles on their faces. They had just not only gotten to ask Cal Ripken a question, but talk with him like anyone else.

Ripken loved being able to do something that involved Aberdeen, especially when it came to baseball. It made everything that much sweeter when there was a ceremony in September 2005 to honor the 10th anniversary of his tying Gehrig's record. Ripken sat in the IronBirds dugout that night, a few minutes before the ceremony and reflected on how happy he was to have this happen in Aberdeen.

"The place that you grow up, the community that you ultimately grow from, was your starting point and having gone on to have a wonderful career and fulfilling a dream, you don't do that all by yourself," Ripken said. "You do it with the help of many people and support. I'm glad we had the chance to celebrate in our community."

The ceremony that night was pure Ripken all the way around. Everything was kept low key and non-flashy as the first part of a two-night celebration of the 10th anniversary of his tying and breaking the record. Everything was done in a reserved manner, from the simple stage placed quietly in the middle of the infield at Ripken Stadium to the festivities that let the sold-out crowd take a look back at what had happened at Oriole Park at Camden Yards the night Cal made history in 1995.

Many of Ripken's family members were onstage with him, along with a few old friends, most notably longtime teammate and friend, Eddie Murray. Ripken always seems like a man in command when talking, but there's a different look to him when he speaks in Aberdeen. It's his hometown. He's one of them. And when he talks, it sounds like a friend talking to friends, not a sports star addressing fans.

"Being in the community, it still astounds me that when I come out to the ballpark that it's not all about the baseball," Ripken said earlier that night. "Maybe it's very little about the baseball; it's an opportunity to gather as a community. You look at all the people in the community, they love to be together, they love to talk, they love to socialize and... this is a community gathering. This is a nice place to kind of reflect and celebrate a moment from someone that came out of Aberdeen."

The laid-back atmosphere is also probably what helps Ripken seem as if he's having more fun. He entered the field for the ceremony wearing a blue IronBirds shirt and black dress pants. But when the ceremony ended, Ripken was to throw the first pitch from the mound to Murray.

That's when the two old teammates began having a little fun. Murray came to the ballpark dressed in a slick tan outfit and walked on the field. The familiar chant of "Ed-die! Ed-die!" broke out from the crowd, and Murray stopped at home plate. Ripken then put on an IronBirds jersey and stood on the rubber. He grinned and told Murray to go into a catcher's crouch. Murray started laughing, was handed a glove, and went down and caught Ripken's pitch.

The two hugged and, for a moment, 10 years ago seemed like last week. It was all about friendship—the kind of thing that small towns love.

Ripken always has credited Murray with being the player who helped him see the right way to do things with the Orioles. Murray wasn't flashy; he didn't say much or look for the spotlight.

Ripken was very similar. He also was not a ballplayer/person who looked for or loved the spotlight. A low-key personality, Ripken found himself under intense pressure throughout the 1995 season as he chased a record many thought could never be broken. Simply put, there were media requests everywhere. The pressure became intense and immense.

But there were many memorable times, signature moments that baseball fans and those in Baltimore will always remember—starting with the number. The team put four numbers on the warehouse wall behind the right field fence and a new number would be unfurled when each game became official in the middle or bottom of the fifth inning. When the team first started doing it during the season, it actually got almost no reaction from the large crowd at Oriole Park. But oh, how that changed.

And by the time Ripken tied and broke the record on consecutive nights in September, the changing of the number had grown into a trademark of the streak. In fact, it remains one of that summer's most memorable things for Baltimore fans. It was not uncommon for fans to stand and cheer when the number would be changed during the games. By summer's end, an ovation was truly a nightly occurrence.

That remained the same at the 10th anniversary celebration of Ripken's breaking the record, one night after the ceremony in Aberdeen. The Orioles put the numbers "2,130" on the warehouse wall at Oriole Park at Camden Yards, and then made the final digit a "1" when the game became official midway through the fifth inning—just as they had done in 1995. The Orioles then brought Ripken onto the field, and both teams and the crowd gave him a standing ovation, just like in 1995.

One of the most memorable moments for everyone that night in 1995 was when Ripken went out of character a bit and took a spontaneous lap around the field, surprising and delighting the crowd. Those few minutes when Ripken basically ran around the warning track, shaking hands with fans and greeting people became one of the most famous moments in Baltimore baseball history. Even the ESPN announcers did something unusual—they remained quiet during the entire episode, letting the pictures speak for themselves.

In fact, Ripken faced more gentle prodding 10 years later when asked if he planned on taking another victory lap. Ripken was very clear about that—"No!" he answered in about five seconds after being asked. It also was very clear that he still felt a bit uncomfortable for having done that lap.

"It was just a wonderful experience," Ripken said of the night 10 years ago. "I fulfilled a dream. I wish I could play for another 3,000 games."

Things were different this time in a number of ways. Ripken didn't take a lap around the field. That night in 1995, against the Angels, he was the Orioles' starting shortstop. This night, he looked more like what he is now—the owner of a minor league baseball team and a businessman— dressed in a dark suit and shirt. He drew a standing ovation as fans gently prodded him to take another lap. But, no, not this time. He smiled but resisted the wishes of the masses.

Ripken is very clear about his feelings of respect for baseball. When he took that victory lap in 1995, thoughts of delaying the game drifted into

his mind. On Tuesday night, he simply waved to the roaring crowd and quietly walked off the field behind home plate.

"That lap was very spontaneous and very out of character for me," he said earlier. "I felt a little ridiculous [at first]. There's no way somebody could've planned that. That was a great experience. It was wonderful to go through. There was genuine excitement."

Ripken drew a standing ovation when introduced to the crowd as he headed out to the field with his family in the pregame ceremonies that night 10 years later. Talking to reporters later, Ripken said he was truly surprised at how much attention came his way for breaking the record.

"I'm still pretty amazed," Ripken said. "I think everyone, in [some] way, wants to leave a mark. It's OK if people remember [that]."

In the end, the ceremonies on those two nights were meant to bring back some of the excitement of 10 years prior in a low-key way. They did just that, and Ripken closed the pregame festivities by hitting all of the right notes with some short remarks.

"Here's to September 6, here's to Camden Yards, and here's to all of you," Ripken told the crowd, drawing another standing ovation.

Ripken doesn't like to call attention to himself, but even he admitted that remembering those two special nights from 1995 was an enjoyable experience.

"It makes you feel good, it makes you feel warm and fuzzy," Ripken said. "I know that any anniversary or a chance to actually reflect [is nice]. It's a nice opportunity to reflect. Eddie came back, which was very special [for] me."

The nights that Ripken tied and broke Gehrig's mark were like a circus in Baltimore. It was an impossible ticket to get, there were 600 to 700 media credentials given out, and the two-night show drew national and international coverage. It grew into something much like a Super Bowl or World Series. After all, Ripken was breaking a record many thought had been truly untouchable.

But Ripken had tried to stay focused and just work on playing throughout that season. The Orioles were struggling around the .500 mark under first-year manager Phil Regan—who lost his job after the year—and Ripken faced constant questions and queries all season long. But he handled everything much like he did on the field, smoothly and gracefully. However, Ripken admitted that the biggest problems for him came in the last days.

"The only pressure was in the last week," Ripken said. "Before that, it was just me, playing baseball, day in and day out."

How huge was the streak? On the night Ripken returned to Camden Yards for the celebration, the Orioles informed the crowd of a small statistic that spoke volumes. Baltimore shortstop Miguel Tejada is much like Ripken in that he's not real big on taking time off. Tejada holds the longest consecutive games streak among active players on that night, with his streak then standing at 894.

The Orioles told the crowd that if Tejada played in every game, he would catch Ripken in July 2016. That fact made the crowd laugh, but it also drove home the enormity of what Ripken did. To Ripken, though, his career and the streak were simply playing out the values that his father and mentors like Eddie Murray taught him.

Ripken is well aware that the streak—which ended at 2,632 games when he quietly took himself out of the lineup about 30 minutes before a home game with New York on September 20, 1998—is going to be the baseball accomplishment he's best known for. He even ended it in a typical Ripken way. The third baseman walked into then-manager Ray Miller's office and told him he wanted the streak to end there. Miller asked Ripken if he was sure and then scratched him from the lineup, putting in prospect Ryan Minor.

The fans didn't even realize it at first, but then Ripken received an ovation early in the game. He also saw the Yankees there on the top step joining in the ovation—a huge sign of respect for a player who truly asked for nothing else but that from teammates and opponents.

"People ask me about the secret; I say that it was about an approach," Ripken said. "It was about a sense of responsibility; it was about doing something that you really love to do. Dad certainly gave me that approach, gave me that sense of responsibility, and he guided me."

Ripken constantly gives credit to his late father, Cal Ripken Sr., for being the driving force and teacher in his baseball career. The elder Ripken died in 1999, but spent many hours working with his kids about how to learn the game he loved when they were little and then pounding home a rather simple message about just giving all you can all of the time when doing something that's meaningful.

"You really need to find something you love and put your all into it, and that's all I did," Ripken said. "I didn't think it was that big of a deal when I played. Dad always thought that was the way a big league baseball player should go about his job, and I did it."

Ripken lived by that standard throughout his big league career—just doing his job. He came up late in the 1981 season after rising through Baltimore's minor league system following his selection in the second round of the 1978 draft. Ripken was both a pitcher and an infielder with Aberdeen High School as a teenager. There actually was some talk within the Orioles organization about making him a pitcher, but he went to the infield.

He struggled badly late in the 1981 season, coming up to the Orioles after the strike split the baseball season into two halves. However, Ripken went just five for 39 (.128)—all singles—in 23 games of limited playing time. But all of that changed the next year. Ripken quickly got regular playing time as the starting third baseman, and the streak began quietly on May 30, 1982, when Weaver put him into the lineup as the No. 8 hitter against the Blue Jays.

Ripken began his record-setting streak of 8,243 innings on June 5 when the Orioles were in Minnesota. But Weaver soon made his big move, shifting Ripken to shortstop when Baltimore played Cleveland on July 1. Nothing bothered Ripken that year as he won the American League Rookie of the Year award with a solid .264 average, 28 homers, and 93 RBI.

His career took off from there, and Ripken became a solid part of the team. Ripken had another big year in 1983 as the Orioles bounced back from losing the American League East in 1982 by one game to take command. They won the division and then beat a tough Chicago team in four games in the American League Championship Series.

The Orioles then won the World Series, beating the Phillies in five games. Ripken even caught the final out, a soft line drive that wrapped up Scott McGregor's 5-0 shutout. Getting the final out was almost something you'd expect, as Ripken played every inning of every game that year and won the American League Most Valuable Player honor after hitting .318 with 27 homers and 102 RBI. He led Major League Baseball with 211 hits.

The streak came close to ending early in the 1985 season when Ripken sprained his left ankle. But the Orioles were off the next day, playing an exhibition game he skipped, and Ripken made it back for the next contest. The streak kept growing, but Ripken found himself answering critics who thought it hampered his performance, especially as the 1980s ended and he struggled a bit.

But he came back in a big way in 1991. That's when Ripken bounced back to win his second American League MVP award, hitting 34 homers with a career-best .323 batting average and 114 RBI. He came close to breaking the streak in game 1,790 in 1993, twisting his knee in a game in Baltimore versus Seattle. The knee became painful and swelled up, but he kept on going. Ripken later told reporters that it was the closest he came to sitting out.

But even though he set so many records, Ripken caught everyone's attention on the nights he tied Gehrig's mark and then broke it. He homered in the sixth inning the first night as the Orioles rolled to an 8-0 win over the Angels. Ripken did it again the following night, homering in the fourth inning of a 4-2 win.

He said that he remembers all of the good things in his career—like the 22-minute ovation he received the night Gehrig's record fell. Ripken said all of that helps him stay balanced now, a few years after retiring, when accolades still come his way.

"I try not to get too carried away with it," Ripken said. "I know I got to do what I wanted for a living, that's play baseball. My dad gave me a sense of responsibility, a way to approach baseball, which was really coming out and being willing to play every day. Eddie Murray [also] showed me the way. Eddie showed me how important it was to be in the lineup."

Ripken often tries to quietly talk down his accomplishments. He's a family businessman now, married to his wife, Kelly, and the father of Rachel and Ryan. He is trying hard to keep up with their lives. The career seemed like it took a long time, and the streak seemed like it lasted forever. But looking back, Ripken says it went by fast—but then he smiles.

"But I enjoyed it thoroughly."

Ripken remains involved in baseball, working a lot locally with the Aberdeen IronBirds minor league team, which has become very popular in the area. He's also been working on a huge number of programs for kids in the Maryland area and other places, things like the Cal Ripken World Series, which brings in teams from around the world.

BRADY ANDERSON

A Different Type of Leadoff Hitter

B rady Anderson was named to the Orioles Hall of Fame during the 2004 season, and his appearance at the ceremony at Oriole Park at Camden Yards was pure Brady.

Everyone associated with the Orioles knew that Anderson did things his way. All the time. He would sometimes roller-blade to the ballpark. He religiously sported a set of long sideburns that he jokingly refused to cut. He would try just about anything to stay in perfect shape. That's just the way it was, and Anderson never changed. He was one of those ballplayers who fans knew by the first name. That's why what happened at the Hall of Fame ceremonies was, well, pure Brady.

It gave a perfect picture of Anderson's iconoclastic personality. Cal Ripken Jr. and others were standing on the stage in the middle of the infield, mostly wearing nice business suits. However, there was Anderson clad in some smooth blue jeans and a shirt, with his trademark slick hair and sideburns, trading laughs and a few sarcastic jokes. Anderson seemed a bit uncomfortable about the whole thing—and those present found out later why.

He still didn't want to admit his playing career was done. When talking with reporters a few minutes after the ceremonies ended, Anderson balked a little when someone asked him about his career in the past tense, as if it were done. Someone else then wondered if Anderson still was thinking about playing.

"I think about it all the time," Anderson said. "I think I can still play. I'm still working."

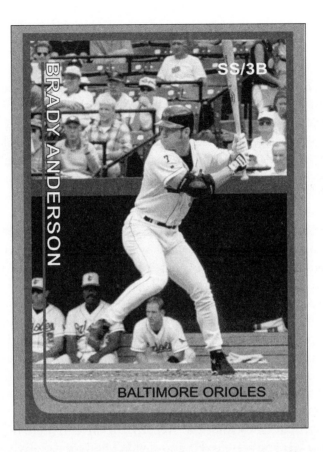

BRADY ANDERSON

SS/3B

BALTIMORE ORIOLES

#9 BRADY ANDERSON • OF
Seasons with the Orioles: 1988-2001

Best Season with the Orioles: 1996
Highlight Stats from that Season: Anderson set a team record by hitting 50 home runs, something rather unusual for a leadoff hitter. He had career highs in homers, RBI (110), average (.297), runs (117), and more, despite missing 13 games and battling some health problems midway through. He also made the All-Star Game that year and ranked second in the American League in homers.

Anderson was honored at Oriole Park a few months after turning 40, and he certainly looked like he still could make a go of it. He had played for Portland in the San Diego system in 2003 and said he loved it. Anderson got released so the Padres could make room for some of their younger players. However, the former outfielder looked good. In fact, it was like he was in better shape than some of the players on the field that day.

It was easy to see in Anderson's eyes that he had been thinking about trying to get back, but the Silver Spring, Maryland, native couldn't do it in 2004 or 2005. He had made the Orioles Hall of Fame, though, something that probably surprised many considering how his career began in Baltimore.

The Orioles knew what they wanted when acquiring Anderson from the Boston Red Sox in a 1988 trade where they gave up starting pitcher Mike Boddicker. They saw a speedy outfielder who could hit some, and they hoped he'd help both offense and defense in the midst of a humiliating 107-loss season.

And although there was no question that the Orioles had acquired a talented player, they weren't quite sure what they had gotten for a while. Anderson struggled the first few years as the Orioles pushed him to be more of a slap and average hitter, something he wasn't really comfortable with and said so many times. But that's what the team thought he'd be good at—even though Anderson wasn't ecstatic with the role.

In fact, Anderson didn't bat over .231 or drive in more than 27 runs during his first four seasons. He also couldn't find regular playing time and never seemed comfortable at the plate, although he often showed his speed and defensive skills in the outfield. However, when then-manager Johnny Oates took the team to spring training in 1992, he made a move that had many scratching their heads.

Oates told Anderson that he'd be the regular leadoff hitter and to basically do what he needed to play his best. Just do it, basically. The move worked as Anderson hit an impressive 21 homers with 80 RBI and a .271 average that season—and it set the tone for the rest of his career. Anderson was a winner with the Orioles after the first few seasons. When Oates showed the faith that made him an everyday player, Anderson blossomed. That same year was when Oriole Park at Camden Yards opened, and Anderson and Cal Ripken quickly became two of the team's most popular players.

But that's when Anderson finally found his niche. After struggling for several seasons to find the right place, Anderson seemed to love playing in the outfield at the new stadium. He ran everywhere and made endless spectacular plays. The fans quickly took to him, and the low-key Anderson didn't want to make a fuss and rarely said much back.

Anderson's most memorable season was 1996 when he belted 50 homers while batting leadoff most of the time. He even made that dramatic, hitting his 50th homer on the season's final day in Toronto. But what many people forget are the problems that Anderson had to battle through to reach that number.

Outside Pitch magazine, a publication that follows the Orioles, did a piece on Anderson when he made the team's Hall of Fame and talked about some of the health troubles he had to face that year—a few of which were very serious.

Anderson had hit 15 homers by May 4, earlier than anyone had ever done it, but a strained quadriceps muscle had forced the outfielder to sit for a few days. Then his season appeared in jeopardy when his appendix flared up around the All-Star break. He appeared destined for surgery but declined and gritted his teeth to play through the rest of the season.

"It would have been kind of easy to listen to the doctors and put my 32-home run, .300 season in the bank," Anderson said in the *Outside Pitch* article. "Even that would have been my best season ever. But then I would have to think, 'What would have happened?' I remember thinking that it just wasn't complete, and I had to find out what I could do."

Anderson found out what he could do, and it was plenty. He kept on swinging and eventually hit that elusive 50th homer. He battled through everything and reached the goal, something impressive for any hitter—and even more so for a leadoff hitter.

In the end, Anderson played 14 seasons with the Orioles, from 1988 to 2001. He was a three-time All-Star who is the club's leader in stolen bases (307), and he set the team record for homers in a season with those 50 he hit in 1996. He and Barry Bonds are the only players in major league history to have a 50-steal and a 50-homer season.

The Orioles released him after a sub-par 2001 season when he hit just .202 in 131 games. Cleveland signed him for 2002, but Anderson played just 34 games there and didn't make it back to the major leagues again.

Staying in such tip-top shape was something that marked Anderson's career. His incredible athletic ability was the other thing that many remember. A few days before Anderson took part in the team's Hall of Fame ceremony, longtime teammate and close friend Cal Ripken Jr. talked about the things that his buddy could do—both on and off the field.

"When I think of Brady, I can't help but think of his athleticism," Ripken said. "He was by far the best athlete I've ever been around. He was

Jesse Orosco, Mike Bordick, and Brady Anderson

challenged on the field and off the field... and competed in everything he did. He wanted to win at everything he did."

But in the end, Anderson simply loved playing at Oriole Park at Camden Yards. Anderson also loved the fans and did something unusual for him on the day he was inducted into the team's Hall of Fame—he spoke directly to those fans.

"It was a thrill playing in such a great ballpark," Anderson said. "Perhaps I did not acknowledge you as much as I [should have], but many times I just wanted to jump into the stands and shake your hands. My only regret was that I was not formally able to say goodbye to you. I'd like to do that now."

Unless, of course, he makes it back to the big leagues again. With Anderson, you never know.

Anderson had been the special assistant to the director of baseball operations with the Orioles, but he recently earned a promotion to vice president of baseball operations and often deals with and helps players with training, staying in shape, and additional baseball activities.

Where Have You Gone?
***

ELROD
HENDRICKS

The Man Everyone Knew

T he story of Elrod Hendricks and what he did before and after his career is an unusual one. Probably a story that would go better in some kind of movie or tribute—especially because of how it ended.

Ellie Hendricks had been part of the Orioles organization for nearly his entire pro career since 1968. He'd been on a baseball field for 45 years and had been told after the 2005 season that he wouldn't be allowed to continue his longtime job as bullpen coach anymore as the Orioles were reassigning him.

That move devastated him. There was no other way to say it. He loved being in uniform and on a baseball field. That's what makes the telling of this story so ironic, emotional, and sad.

I had tried to interview Hendricks several times over the 2005 season and a half, but scheduling problems kept screwing things up—and I had pretty much given up when I found out that he'd be the Santa Claus at a party the Orioles threw for underprivileged children in downtown Baltimore the week before Christmas this past winter. We talked for a little while that cold Monday afternoon, and it was easy to see how frustrated he was with not being able to go on the field anymore. The team hadn't let him know what his role was going to be, but he wasn't looking forward to the 2006 season.

"It's definitely [going to be] very difficult because I've been on the field for 45 years," Hendricks said. "I don't feel that... right now. Once spring training begins, it's going to be difficult for me. I've even thought many times, how hard it was watching the Orioles play on TV [when I was sick in 2005], I can't imagine that it's going to be any better. So I probably, at

41

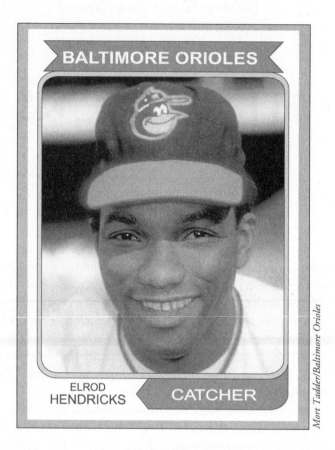

BALTIMORE ORIOLES

ELROD
HENDRICKS

CATCHER

#10 ELROD HENDRICKS • C
Years with the Orioles: 1968-1972, 1973-1976, 1978-1979

Best Season with the Orioles: 1970
Highlight Stats from that Season: The Orioles used Hendricks's help
to win their second World Series in five seasons. Hendricks tied a career-high with 12 homers and had a career-best 41 RBI. He then crushed
a clutch solo homer in Game 1 of the World Series that helped the Orioles
rally for a 4-3 victory over the Reds and added a clutch
hit the following day in Game 2.

least right now, am thinking of not even turning on and watching the game or listening to the game. I'll see what happens afterward. It's going to be difficult."

Then, two days later, just a few days before Christmas, he died suddenly, one day before his 65th birthday. It was a death that sent shockwaves through the Baltimore community. Callers flooded the radio talk shows with stories of his generosity and kindness. He would never miss talking to a kid, answering a question, or signing an autograph. Hendricks ran one of the Baltimore area's most respected baseball camps.

Kids played hard if they went there. But they learned a lot. And Hendricks was always there if the Orioles were in town. He'd be there, often in uniform, to talk to kids who wanted to make the major leagues. Hendricks also would do little things like bring surprise visitors, such as Eddie Murray. These weren't things that were advertised. Hendricks just did them.

That's why he was so frustrated and broken by what the Orioles did. The pain in his voice was obvious that day. He still wanted to be on the field, but the Orioles were concerned about his health. Hendricks was 64 and had had a mild stroke that kept him out for about 18 games early in 2005. The team felt the travel could wear him down, so they said they were reassigning him.

He still was helping the team with community affairs, however, as he always did. That's why he was at the Christmas party that day. Before dressing up as Santa Claus and letting all of the children sit on his lap, Hendricks acted as a waiter to serve a large group of children. He delighted the kids with his booming voice and loud laughter.

"It's a joy to watch the faces, the smiles, watching them open the gifts," Hendricks said that day. "It's a warm feeling. It's easy for me to be involved. It takes me back to being a kid, too. I hear some funny things and have to hold back my laughter."

Maybe being part of the Orioles was what meant so much to Hendricks because he'd been with the team for so long. Hendricks played for the Orioles much of his major league career. All but 53 of the 711 major league games he played in from 1968 to 1979 came as an Oriole, and Hendricks became a fixture in this town. Hendricks served an interesting role with the Orioles for a long time, often alternating with Andy Etchebarren to form a tough catching duo.

Etchebarren was a solid defensive catcher, who could get big hits. Hendricks was different, a left-handed dead-pull hitter who could crush some pitches. Hendricks came to the Orioles in a Rule V transaction deal before 1968 after playing in the minors for the Braves, Cardinals, and Angels. Earl

Weaver, who took over as the manager midway through the 1968 season, pushed to get Hendricks a spot on the roster, and it happened that year.

The Orioles benefited greatly from his timely power hitting. Although he never hit more than 12 homers in a season, they seemed to come at good times. Hendricks hit a clutch homer in Game 1 of the 1970 World Series, helping the Orioles rally from an early 3-0 deficit to pull out a 4-3 win over Cincinnati. His round-tripper came leading off the fifth inning and tied the game at 3-3. Brooks Robinson's solo shot won the game later on.

Hendricks also was involved in one of the stranger plays in the Series in the sixth inning. With the game still tied, the Reds put runners on first and third with one out. Pinch hitter Ty Cline then hit a Baltimore chop right in front of home plate. Hendricks grabbed the ball and tagged runner Bernie Carbo at home. Home plate umpire Ken Burkhart got a little too close to the play and got turned around but called Carbo out. Replays later showed that while Hendricks indeed tagged Carbo—but he had the ball in the other hand.

The Reds then took a 4-0 lead in Game 2 and knocked out Orioles ace Mike Cuellar early, but Hendricks came up with another big hit, poking an RBI double off reliever Milt Wilcox down the left field line to complete a five-run fifth inning and give the Orioles a 6-4 lead. Baltimore later held on to win 6-5. Robinson jokingly said later that it might have been the only time he saw Hendricks hit a ball to the opposite field. The Orioles eventually won that Series in five games.

They suffered a painful seven-game loss to Pittsburgh in the 1971 World Series, but Hendricks had a good run, going five for 19 then. Hendricks was traded to the Cubs in a late 1972 deal, but came back to Baltimore the next year. He was traded to the Yankees in a big 1976 trade, but came back to Baltimore to end his career after staying in New York through the 1977 season.

Hendricks became the bullpen coach who played occasionally (13 games) in 1978 and became an even bigger part of the community. He always had been one of the players the team could count on to go out and work with anything involving children, but he took it to another level after becoming a coach. Hendricks truly became an ambassador for the team. He could be seen everywhere, but he wasn't a person who simply did things to look good in front of a camera. In fact, many of Hendricks's good deeds were in quiet hospital rooms when no one was around.

A perfect example involves a Baltimore resident who saw her child die a slow and painful death from cancer at the age of 17 in 1982. Hendricks met the child and the two became friends. He made repeated trips to the hospital to see him and urged him to keep fighting, take his medicine, and try, something that proved valuable when the boy was especially down. Hendricks also gave him a signed Orioles cap that the family has 23 years later. This wasn't a phone call in front of the cameras that just looked good.

Family members still get emotional when bringing up Hendricks's name and couldn't stop shaking their heads at a holiday party a few days after he died. It wasn't hard to find stories of Hendricks and his kindness. People who had no business with the Orioles and would remember just one small thing he did at one time. One story is about a boy who went to Hendricks's camp one summer day to drop something off to someone and was struck by how kind he was in helping a player who'd been struggling on the field. He saw Hendricks pull the child off to the side, sit him on a rock, and tell him not to quit, to keep trying and working, and he'd get better. The child ran back on to field as if shot from a cannon with a memory that would stay alive forever.

That was Elrod Hendricks.

Curt Motton and Elrod Hendricks became very close, creating a friendship Motton took pride in until the day the former Orioles catcher/coach died.

While eulogizing Hendricks at his funeral, Motton talked and laughed about how two people who were so different could grow into such good friends. Motton smiled when talking how Hendricks and he were truly so different. He talked about how he was a righty, and Hendricks was left-handed. Hendricks liked to stand close to the plate; Motton "couldn't get far enough away," and they each favored different kinds of pitches.

But Motton said he'd never forget about how Hendricks helped so many in the Baltimore community in nearly four decades in town.

"[He] really touched people's hearts," Motton said. "Making them feel good about themselves, giving them hope."

DOUG DeCINCES

Replacing a Legend with Class, Part I

Doug DeCinces made his way into the majors and found himself facing the hardest and most thankless job of all—replacing a legend. But he did it with style and class and became a very good ballplayer in his own right.

The Orioles picked DeCinces in the third round of the 1970 draft, and he quickly had a strong minor league stint. DeCinces made his way to the majors for good in 1974 when Brooks Robinson was at the tail end of his career.

The six-foot-two Californian earned the starting job for good in 1976, and Robinson retired later during the 1977 season. Many people wondered how the low-key DeCinces could stand the heat of replacing the legend. Baltimoreans had seen how difficult that could be a few years before when Marty Domres replaced Johnny Unitas as the starting quarterback for the Colts, and that didn't go very well.

But DeCinces handled the pressure with cool and calm, despite the fact that no matter what he did, Baltimore fans seemed to want to be angry at him. Talking about it 28 years after the fact, DeCinces just smiled.

"I look back now and probably one of the things I'm most proud of in my career is replacing Brooks Robinson," DeCinces said. "To survive it and go on and have my own career and still establish myself here with the Orioles. Brooks is such a fabulous baseball player and a fabulous human being. Everyone loved him so much."

DeCinces knew exactly where he stood when taking over for Robinson, who had slowly been sliding since having a big year in 1971. Robinson had had more and more trouble at the plate each year, and DeCinces was be-

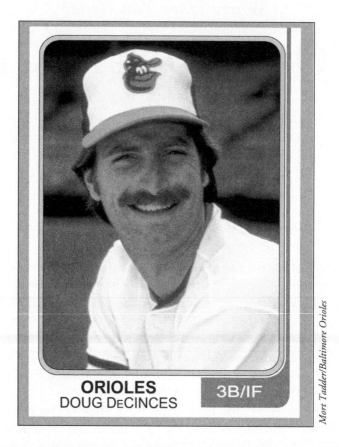

ORIOLES
DOUG DeCINCES

3B/IF

Mort Tadder/Baltimore Orioles

#11 DOUG DeCINCES • 3B/IF
Seasons with the Orioles: 1973-1981

Best Season with the Orioles: 1978
Highlight Stats from that Season: DeCinces showed plenty of punch in his bat during the first year after Brooks Robinson retired. He had 28 homers with 80 RBI and a .286 batting average, finishing third in the American League in slugging percentage (.526) and second in extra-base hits (66).

ing projected—correctly as it turned out—as a big-time power hitter who could give the Orioles another strong bat in the lineup.

But it was the defensive side of things that caused DeCinces some trouble. He was a solid third baseman in the field, but anytime he did anything wrong, the Robinson comparisons would start. If DeCinces made a few bad plays, the local radio talk shows would have fans saying over and over again, "Brooks wouldn't have done that." Orioles fans kept saying things like that even though DeCinces was giving Baltimore more offense than Robinson had given the team during his final four years as a starter.

"I was kind of in a no-win situation," DeCinces said. "I had to overcome a lot of things. Just being able to survive that, really just because of the honor of what everyone thought of Brooks. I didn't take it personally [even though] I used to get hate mail and a bunch of stuff."

DeCinces had struggled his last few years in Baltimore. After a career high of 28 homers and 80 RBI plus a .286 average in 1978, his numbers slowly slid down. He played in only 100 games in 1981—thanks to the midseason players' strike—and finished with 13 homers and 55 RBI along with a .263 batting average. Some wondered if DeCinces was going to develop into a major power hitter because he seemed to be averaging around 15 homers a year for the Orioles, and his average had slipped a bit.

Interestingly, the Orioles traded him to the Angels after the 1981 season as part of a deal for outfielder Dan Ford. But the trade to the Angels seemed to be a breakthrough for DeCinces, who took off once he went back home to California. He became an All-Star and one of the game's most respected and consistent players. The Orioles did win the World Series in 1983— with Ford coming up with one of the big hits against the Phillies, but the team went through a seeming revolving door at third base for several years after DeCinces left.

"I got traded to the Angels and then I came back, and they didn't have anybody playing third," DeCinces said. "I don't know, [there were] 40 different guys. I kind of felt like the artist who became famous after he died."

DeCinces was right in the fact that Baltimore used numerous players at third base, and it took the team several years to find someone who made the pitchers and everyone else relaxed—both in hitting and fielding skills. The fact that Robinson was such an incredible fielder made many overlook the fact that DeCinces became a solid defensive player.

"I remember Scott McGregor and Mike Flanagan saying they were not comfortable throwing their change-up after [I left]," DeCinces said.

DeCinces's career truly took off when he joined the Angels. His big year was 1982 with 30 homers and 97 RBI along with a .301 batting average.

He played a big role in helping California to the American League Championship Series before the Angels wasted a 2-0 series lead against the Milwaukee Brewers. The Brewers won the final three games and advanced to the World Series, where they lost to the St. Louis Cardinals in a nail-biting seven-game battle.

Interestingly, DeCinces made his only All-Star appearance the following year. He finished with 18 homers and 65 RBI in just 95 games and a .281 batting average before injuries slowed him.

DeCinces later worked in real estate development and golf. He nearly got back into baseball and would have if a different group had bought the Angels several years ago.

DeCinces had another connection with the Orioles' organization around the turn of the century when his son, Tim, played in their minor league system. A good left-handed hitter who was a catcher, Tim DeCinces didn't fare quite as well as his dad and never got a shot at the major league level. DeCinces said his son learned one of life's harder lessons from baseball.

"He's working with me now in the real estate business and doing very well," DeCinces said with a smile. "He did everything he could and just didn't quite get there. He was knocking on that door and sometimes that door doesn't open to get to the big leagues. Sometimes people don't realize how difficult it is."

DeCinces got his appreciation in Baltimore later on, specifically at the end of the 2004 season, when he was picked as one of the 50 most popular players in the franchise's first 50 years. He came to Oriole Park at Camden Yards, and it was easy to see how much he enjoyed being back where his career began.

"I was very lucky to have the career I had," DeCinces said. "I look back at the people who were really influential in my career, and I can't say enough about Cal Ripken Sr. He was my baseball dad. He helped me so much as a player in the minor leagues, and that's what allowed me to be successful in the big leagues."

DeCinces made news off the field the last few years after being charged in an insider trading scandal in 2012. He was indicted in federal court in California (Santa Ana), according to numerous reports, and charged with getting $1.3 million in profits through insider trading. He paid $2.5 million a few months earlier to settle a Securities and Exchange Commission civil lawsuit involving the same company.

TOMMY DAVIS

The First Designated Hitter

N early 30 years after his baseball career ended, Tommy Davis often could be found talking about it somewhere.

Even though Davis was the Orioles' first designated hitter and played in Baltimore for a little more than three years, his greatest days came in Los Angeles, when he grew into one of baseball's most feared hitters. His 1962 season was one for the books, when he hit .346 with 27 homers and 153 RBI. Davis played with the Dodgers from 1959 to 1966, but a dislocated ankle suffered in 1965 slowed him badly.

However, he's kept busy after his baseball career, often doing things involving the sport. He's a very active speaker about the Dodgers and baseball in the Southern California area. He's a member of the Dodgers Speakers Bureau and will often be found talking at different spots and putting on his old No. 12 jersey.

But even though Davis's most memorable days came with the Dodgers, he made some history in Baltimore. Davis came to the Orioles in what looked like a kind of throwaway deal with the Chicago Cubs.

The trade didn't look like much on paper. Seemingly swapping a pair of hitters on the downside of their respective careers, the Cubs sent outfielder/first baseman Davis to the Orioles for catcher Ellie Hendricks on August 18, 1972. Both players were in the midst of terrible seasons, and the deal didn't get much attention. The Orioles were desperately looking for someone who could help them on offense. Baltimore was in the midst of one of the worst seasons at the plate in team history, but still had a shot at the American League East title.

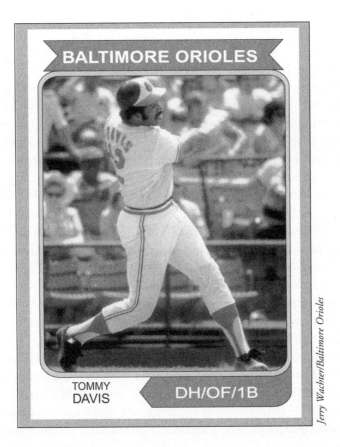

BALTIMORE ORIOLES

TOMMY
DAVIS

DH/OF/1B

Jerry Wachter/Baltimore Orioles

#12 TOMMY DAVIS • DH/OF/1B
Seasons with the Orioles: 1972-1975

Best Season with the Orioles: 1974
Highlight Stats from that Season: Davis finished with 11 homers and 84
RBI with a .289 batting average in 158 games. His consistent work as a
designated hitter helped the Orioles win the American League East
for the second straight year.

The Orioles came up short that season, but that deal turned out big. The designated hitter rule was put in place in the American League for the 1973 season. Davis took over as the full-time designated hitter when the new position was instituted. The DH extended Davis's career four more seasons after the right-handed hitter showed that his bat still had plenty of pop even though he was 34 years old at the start of the 1973 season.

Davis wasn't sure where he was going after the 1972 season. He said the Orioles sent him a Class AAA contract, and Davis was set to go to Japan. But then he heard about the designated hitter.

"It was the first year that they were going to have the DH," Davis said. "I found out they were going to have the DH, so I called them up and said that I'd like to go to spring training with the major league team if I can, so they honored me with that, and I made the team in spring training."

However, he fit in perfectly with the Orioles in 1973. The Orioles had missed the playoffs in 1972 after winning three straight American League East and American League titles, along with a World Series crown in 1970. They didn't want a repeat of the poor offensive performance of 1972 and were hoping Davis could help—and he did.

Davis was the DH in 127 games as the Orioles bounced back to win the East Division before falling to Oakland in the league championship series. He finished third in the American League with a .306 average plus seven homers and 89 RBI, serving as a rock for an Orioles team that had a mix of older and younger players. Davis also finished 10th in the Most Valuable Player voting.

He posted even better numbers in 1974 when the Orioles won the AL East once more. Davis played 158 games—155 at DH—and batted .289 with 11 homers and 84 RBI, ending up among the league leaders in several offensive categories. Davis belted out 181 hits, tied for the second-most number of hits he ever finished with in a season, but the Orioles fell again to Oakland in the ALCS. He also hit .286 and .267 during the two championship series battles with Oakland.

Davis's final year as the Orioles' designated hitter came in 1975 when he played in 116 games and hit .283 with six homers and 57 RBI. The Orioles released him before the 1976 season, and he finished the season with the Angels and Royals before retiring. But the designated hitter proved to be a big plus for Davis, and he knows it.

"I did love being [the DH]," Davis said. "I had a lot of fun doing it, too."

Davis loves to tell one story of his life as a designated hitter. He was talking to his first wife on the clubhouse phone when trainer Ralph Salvon came over and tapped him on the shoulder.

"I said, 'What do you need?' And he said, 'You're up, right now,'" Davis said with a laugh. "I had to go all the way through the tunnel, and [manager] Earl [Weaver] was there with those strange little eyes. I think I got a base hit, and I knocked in a run. I came back, and I had to go through the tunnel, and he wouldn't look at me. He looked the other way."

Davis paused for a moment and smiled.

"And then I finished the conversation on the phone," he said with a laugh.

He took pride in being both the first designated hitter in Orioles history and a player who helped Baltimore win consecutive division titles in 1973 and 1974. Davis truly was a big help for the Orioles because his bat kept many innings going and gave the team a number of key hits. The designated hitter looked like it truly was built for someone like Davis, and the Orioles were the ones who reaped the benefits.

Davis was honored by the city of Rancho Cucamonga (California) in the summer of 2013 for his career success and community service. He's been living there for over 30 years and is very popular in that community, where he does a lot of work with baseball and children.

JEFF MANTO

A Real Hit

The Pittsburgh Pirates hired Jeff Manto to be their hitting coach for the 2006 season in late November 2005. He knows a lot about hitting. But there's probably little doubt about the finest moments of Manto's big league career—something that, of course, involved hitting.

The utility player who toiled for several clubs had his best season with the Orioles in 1995 and set a franchise record that still stands today when he homered in four consecutive official at-bats.

The funny part is that Manto didn't realize what was happening when it happened.

Manto also tied a major league record because he homered in his previous game, tying Johnny Blanchard of the 1964 New York Yankees as the only players to hit five homers in three games. But Manto didn't realize that either record had happened.

"It took three days, and nobody ever said anything," said Manto, now 49 and formerly Pittsburgh's minor league hitting coordinator. "It was pretty cool. It was something I'll never forget—but I never knew what the hell was going on."

Manto started everything by homering off Solomon Torres in his first at-bat on June 8 against Seattle. He then flew out to left off of Rafael Carmona before blasting a three-run homer in his final at-bat on a 1-0 curveball that helped the Orioles lock up a victory.

Manto got into the lineup again the following day against the Angels. He hit a two-run homer in his first at-bat off starter Russ Springer in the second inning and walked in his next two times up. Manto then homered in the sixth again off Springer, as the Orioles rolled to a 10-4 victory. Man-

JEFF MANTO

3B/1B/DH

BALTIMORE ORIOLES

#12 JEFF MANTO • 3B/1B/DH
Seasons with the Orioles: 1995

Highlight Stats from that Season: It was his only year with Baltimore, and Manto had his best season anywhere. Manto finished with 17 homers and 38 RBI in 89 games and batted .256. He was a surprise power hitter that the Orioles benefited from in a big way, and Manto set a team record with four homers in four straight official at-bats.

to went two for two in the game with walks in the other two appearances.

The streak continued in Manto's next game, June 10 against the Angels. He blasted a solo homer off Mike Bielecki for a home run on a fourth straight at-bat. Manto then walked in the fourth before making an out on his next at-bat by flying out to deep center on a 3-0 pitch.

That's when Manto realized something was up. He went out to third base, where Cal Ripken Jr. handed him his glove and then looked up at the scoreboard, hoping to see a replay of his swing, as players often do. But instead of a replay, Manto saw the message saying that he'd hit a home run on four consecutive at-bats.

And he was shocked.

"Apparently the [players] knew something," Manto said with a laugh. "Cal was up on everything, but being the class act that he was, he kept his mouth shut."

Ripken, also being the detail-oriented person that he was, had a question for Manto upon handing him his glove after the fly out.

"Why did you swing on 3-0?" he asked.

Manto still laughs when talking about how he simply didn't realize what was going on. He wasn't quite sure how it happened, but he didn't know that he was making history.

"I was surprised and obviously very humbled also," Manto said.

The 1995 season was Manto's best in the major leagues. He set career highs in nearly every category, hitting 17 homers with 38 RBI in 89 games. Manto played with seven other teams over a total of nine seasons, but never again had more than three homers or 14 RBI. He also enjoyed the season because he got to be a part of Ripken's record-breaking consecutive game streak.

Manto played the night that Ripken tied Lou Gehrig's record of 2,130 consecutive games. He even helped in the Orioles' 8-0 victory over the Angels by blasting a solo homer in a four-run second inning. In fact, he was one of four Baltimore hitters who homered in that inning.

"To do it that year, with the great stuff Cal was doing, I couldn't draw up a better scenario," Manto said.

Manto credited his success that year to then-manager Phil Regan not being afraid to take a chance on him. Regan often would place him between tough hitters Harold Baines and Kevin Bass. That let Manto see a number of good pitches, because pitchers didn't want to deal with Baines and Bass too much that year. Manto would bat sixth or seventh and sometimes even fifth—often getting the right pitches to hit.

"I think I was one of those fortunate guys who could hide in the lineup," Manto said. "It was one of those things where, from a baseball standpoint,

I couldn't have been in a better situation."

Manto nearly duplicated the feat when playing for the Cleveland's Class AAA Buffalo affiliate—about two years later. He hit three homers in a row and was going for the fourth but struck out swinging at an eye-high fastball on a full count.

"This time I knew," he said with a laugh. "I swung at a 3-2 fastball and completely missed it."

Manto played some more time in the minors and eventually wound up playing all or parts of nine seasons in the majors from 1990 to 2000 with the Indians, Phillies, Orioles, Red Sox, Mariners, Tigers, Yankees, and Rockies. He finished his career with 31 homers, 97 RBI, and a .230 average.

He stayed in baseball after leaving the Orioles and then the majors. Manto went on to become a coach with Philadelphia's Class A Lakewood team in 2001. He became the manager of that team in 2002. After that, Manto came to the Pirates in October 2002 as a roving hitting instructor and was very well respected by the team. He then was added to the Pittsburgh coaching staff for the end of the 2005 season after the minor leagues ended play. Then, when Jim Tracy came from Los Angeles to take over as manager for the 2006 season, he named Manto the hitting coach.

"Jeff has done a real good job for us since he has been here," Pittsburgh general manager Dave Littlefield told MLB.com when Manto was promoted. "He's a very hard worker. He has an effervescent personality that is combined with the fact that he's had a lot of experience at a variety of levels. He understands the major leagues. But yet, particularly with a lot of young players that we have, he relates well to the group we have."

Manto's experience with some of the younger players in the Pittsburgh system proved to be a key reason why he got the job, even though Tracy brought in some other coaches when moving over from Los Angeles.

"Jim Tracy and I talked about a lot of different candidates and talked to some different people," Littlefield told MLB.com. "We certainly researched thoroughly in regards to people we had interest in. [Jeff] has worked with a lot of our hitters who have come through the minor leagues and have been successful. That's something that did come into play. I think this is a guy... who is very well respected."

Manto was hired by the Orioles in 2013 as their minor league hitting coordinator. Previously, he had served as the White Sox hitting coach, starting in 2012 under new manager Robin Ventura. From 2008 to 2011, he worked as the organization's minor league hitting coordinator. Previously, he worked with Pittsburgh, serving as the Pirates' hitting coach in 2006 and 2007.

Where Have You Gone?

MIKE BORDICK

Replacing a Legend with Class, Part II

M ike Bordick found himself in an unusual position during the 2004 baseball season—out of the game. But that was just fine with him.

Bordick had experienced plenty of good things in baseball during a career that lasted 1,720 games and included two trips to the World Series and three to a league championship series. But he spent the summer of 2004 doing something that he loved—being with his kids.

The shortstop who replaced Orioles legend Cal Ripken Jr. enjoyed simply being a father. Bordick and his wife have five children and have remained in the Baltimore area. They have four boys and one girl, a fact that keeps the parents rather occupied.

"I'm doing a lot of car pooling," Bordick said with a grin. "It's an active house. I definitely want to spend more time with my family. That window of opportunity with the kids doesn't last very long."

Bordick was concerned about taking advantage of that opportunity, because his oldest child was 12 in 2005. That's another reason he began doing some Little League coaching in the summer of 2004. His son's team made the playoffs and enjoyed themselves, making Bordick a happy coach. The former Oriole used that summer as a bit of a transition period while he was starting to figure out what to do with the rest of his life.

"I certainly wanted to keep my hand in the game," Bordick said. "I learned from some great people."

Bordick started his career with the strong Oakland A's teams of the early 1990s. He made his first major league appearance during the 1990 season where Oakland made its third consecutive trip to the World Series. Bordick credits a lot of his success to learning from a strong group of veteran players

61

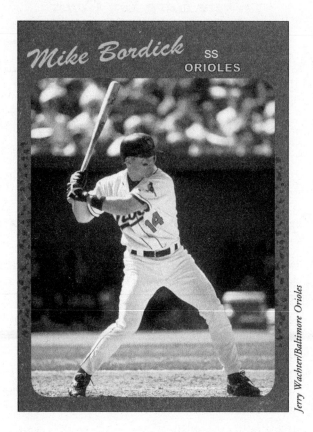

Jerry Wachter/Baltimore Orioles

#14 MIKE BORDICK • SS
Seasons with the Orioles: 1997-2000 and 2001-2002

Best Season with the Orioles: 2000
Highlight Stats from that Season: Even though he got traded to the Mets on July 28, Bordick hit 16 homers and had 59 RBI in just 100 games for the Birds. That was the only season he made the All-Star Game, and the Mets wanted him for their stretch run to the playoffs.

that helped the A's become arguably the top team in baseball during that time period.

"First of all, I was probably the luckiest player in the world to be able to play with the Oakland A's [then]," Bordick said. "People like [manager Tony] La Russa, Carney [Lansford], [Dave] Stewart, the list goes on and on of people whom I learned from. That was probably the most influential."

Bordick enjoyed a strong five-year run as a starter with Oakland before coming to Baltimore as a free agent before the 1997 season. Signing with the Orioles could have been a ticklish situation because the team wanted him to come and take over as the starting shortstop with Ripken moving to third base. Bordick and Ripken talked before the deal was done to make sure everyone was comfortable with the move. The low-key personality that Bordick brought to the table probably was helpful, because asking a long-time starter to move can be dicey. But the move worked just fine.

"Fortunately Cal is a great person and helped make that transition smooth for me," Bordick said. "It also helped that year that we had so much success on the field."

The Orioles turned it on in 1997 after making the playoffs as a wild card team the year before. They won the American League East crown, leading from wire to wire for the club's first division title in 14 years. Bordick played a big role in that, giving the Orioles the solid play they needed up the middle, and as the shortstop combined with second baseman Roberto Alomar to give the team a strong double-play combination.

Bordick also found something different upon becoming an Oriole—power at the plate. The five-foot-11, 175-pound shortstop hadn't hit more than eight homers in a season before taking off in 1998. He hit 13 homers that season and added 10 homers plus a career-high 77 RBI in 1999. During the first 100 games of the 2000 season, Bordick took off, hitting 16 homers and driving in 59 runs with a .297 average, making his first All-Star team.

But the business of baseball hit that summer. The New York Mets, looking for more infield help, traded for Bordick on July 28. They gave the Orioles three players who didn't accomplish much along with infielder Melvin Mora, a man who never had been able to find a consistent position. Mora has wound up playing for the Orioles ever since, and when Bordick rejoined the team as a free agent before the following season, the deal wound up to be a major steal for the Orioles, something that helped the team for several years.

Jim Gentile, Mike Bordick, Boog Powell, Scott McGregor, and Mike Boddicker

He played two more years in Baltimore before signing with Toronto as a free agent before the 2003 season. Bordick ended his career on a good note, batting .274 while playing a few different positions for the Blue Jays.

Bordick then worked at becoming a very busy father following his retirement that winter. He spent plenty of time taking his kids around the area but still had an interest in doing something in baseball.

Coaching Little League baseball was enjoyable to him that first spring after the end of his playing days. His team didn't win the championship, but he had a lot of fun doing it.

"It was a learning experience for me," Bordick said with a laugh. "I guess I'll start at the bottom and work my way up."

He served as a Special Assignment Instructor for the Orioles last season and also works as an analyst on some of the team's TV broadcasts.

SCOTT McGREGOR

The Crafty Lefty

S cott McGregor was the kind of pitcher every manager loves. He was a crafty left-hander who knew how to throw strikes, rarely got into trouble, and was a winner. McGregor pitched in a number of huge games for the Orioles and usually threw well, posting a winning record for eight straight years in Baltimore.

But McGregor left baseball after retiring early in the 1988 season. A religious man, he went into the ministry for 14 years and got to work with and help people along with spending lots of time with his family, time that he used to make up for the time he was away with the Orioles during his major league career. However, McGregor had a bit of a baseball itch that he could never quite make go away.

"In the back of my mind, I always wanted to come back and work with kids in the minor leagues," McGregor said.

And he finally did just that, going back to the Orioles to become a minor league pitching coach starting in the 2002 season. He joined his old friends to help some of the young pitchers the team had in its system. McGregor has been very successful as a coach, working with Aberdeen (Cal Ripken Jr.'s team) for one year in its short season before going to Frederick and staying there for three years. The Keys' pitchers were outstanding for three years and helped the team win the Class A Carolina League championship in 2005.

After that success, the Orioles moved McGregor up to Class AA Bowie to follow some of the young pitchers they're counting on to help the team grow again.

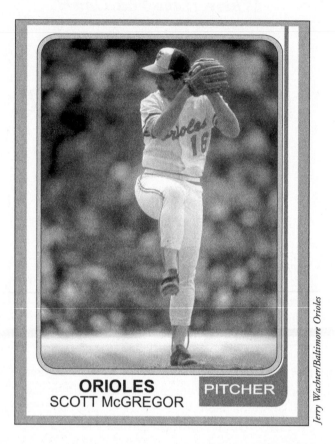

ORIOLES
SCOTT McGREGOR

PITCHER

#16 SCOTT McGREGOR • P
Years with the Orioles: 1976-1988

Best Season with the Orioles: 1980
Highlight Stats from that Season: This was McGregor's lone 20-win season. The left-hander went 20-8 with a 3.32 ERA with 12 complete games for good measure. He might have done it again in 1981, but the strike cut short the season, and McGregor finished 13-5.

"I love it; I really do," McGregor said. "I have a blast. I get to go to big league camp with the guys. They're good, and now we're starting to see some fruit. We've got a lot of good pitchers in the system, and it's very rewarding."

He was well respected and liked by the minor leaguers he worked with, who had no trouble listening to someone who pitched in the majors for more than a decade.

But the interesting thing to McGregor was finding out that no matter how much things had changed, they seemed to stay the same.

"I think the biggest surprise that I probably found after being out for 14 years was the same things I talked about with [Mike] Flanagan and Jim Palmer is what they're still talking about today," McGregor said. "The game itself on the field doesn't change. Kids are quicker, the thing I don't like is they rush them too quickly nowadays."

McGregor said he's seen that a lot of things haven't changed. He said the way pitchers are worked remains the same. But things have changed in other ways as situational pitching has become the norm rather than the exception.

"You've got a lot more starters who don't have to go nine innings," Mc-Gregor said. "If you've got guys out there who are qualified, they're making too much money nowadays not to use them."

McGregor won two of the biggest games in Orioles history. He locked up the 1979 American League Championship Series by shutting out the Angels 8-0 in Game 4 of the best-of-five series. He also clinched the 1983 World Series by blanking the Phillies 5-0 in Game 5, making sure the Orioles didn't blow a three-games-to-one lead like they did against Pittsburgh four years earlier.

The 1979 ALCS win meant a lot to McGregor because he pitched it in Anaheim in front of family and friends—he's from Inglewood, a nearby town. The Angels had a little bit of momentum that day, having won Game 4 the night before with a strange two-run rally in the ninth that was capped by Orioles center fielder Al Bumbry's error.

But the Angels did nothing with McGregor then. The left-hander scattered six hits and struck out four, going the distance in the easy win. The Orioles broke the game open with a five-run seventh inning.

"I pitched that clincher in Anaheim in front of my family, and that was great," McGregor said.

But the Orioles couldn't close out Pittsburgh in the World Series that followed. Baltimore jumped out to a three-games-to-one lead—with Mc-Gregor winning one of those games—before the Pirates suddenly came to

life and won the final three games. Baltimore scored just two runs over the final three games as the Pirates scored wins of 7-1, 4-0, and 4-1.

In Game 7 McGregor had a 1-0 lead when Rich Dauer hit a solo homer, and Willie Stargell's two-run homer in the sixth gave the Pirates the lead for good. McGregor gave up two runs on seven hits in a strong eight-inning stint, but the Orioles' bats went cold at the wrong time.

Those were some of the things that were on McGregor's mind when the Orioles won Game 4 of the 1983 Series to take a three-games-to-one lead over the Phillies. He said he'd already seen the Orioles become an answer to a trivia question he'd rather not have known the answer to—how many teams have blown a three-games-to-one lead in the World Series.

"I dealt with that the night before [Game 4 in 1983]," he said. "Here we were, up 3-1, and I said, 'Lord, we can't be the only team in history to do this twice.' I battled with that all night and finally, I just said in the middle of the night, 'That's it. I'm just going to go out there tomorrow, and I'm going to just do my thing and pitch.'"

McGregor did his thing just fine and shut down the strong Philadelphia lineup. He got some help from teammates Eddie Murray (two homers) and Rick Dempsey (one more), and had a 5-0 lead in the fifth inning. That let McGregor settle in, and he had little trouble in getting the championship-clinching win.

"Eddie hit his home run early [second inning], and they gave me five runs early," McGregor said. "It just took all the pressure off of me."

He began to struggle a little after that, giving up more home runs (34 and 35 in 1985 and 1986 for an Orioles team that was starting to slide downward). McGregor then slid to 2-7 in 1987 and was 0-3 when the Orioles released him in early May 1988, ending his career.

McGregor still keeps a good viewpoint of things. He ended with a career record of 138-108, all with the Orioles, who were actually lucky to get him. The Yankees made McGregor a first-round draft pick in the 1972 draft, but traded him to Baltimore in the June 1976 blockbuster trade that served the Orioles well for a long time.

Baltimore got McGregor, Rick Dempsey, and Tippy Martinez, along with pitchers Rudy May and Dave Pagan. They helped for a short stretch, and the team had only given up Doyle Alexander and Ken Holtzman, starters who were on the downside of their careers; reliever Grant Jackson; and catcher Elrod Hendricks (who later came back to the team) plus a minor leaguer.

McGregor broke in late in 1976 with three appearances, became a spot starter the following year before becoming a part of the rotation for good in 1978 and staying for the next several years.

"Just getting to the big leagues in 1976 was a trip," McGregor said. "And to have two World Series in your career, well, it was pretty special."

And that's why McGregor's glad to be back in a uniform again.

McGregor joined the Orioles as their bullpen coach in the summer of 2013, when pitching coach Rick Adair took a personal leave of absence and bullpen coach Bill Castro took Adair's job. In 2014, McGregor will be back to working with minor leaguers again.

LARRY SHEETS

Still Playing Games

L arry Sheets hasn't played in Major League Baseball since 1993 when he had a cup of coffee with the Seattle Mariners. But sports have remained a big part of his life—in a different way.

Sheets opened up the Larry Sheets Players Family Amusement Center in Westminster, Maryland (Carroll County), a 15,000-square-foot indoor sports arena that offers children and adults a little bit of everything. It's become very popular in the area and often draws players and teams from other places. Sheets also gives lessons about baseball—something he knows plenty about especially because he spent six full years plus parts of two more in the majors, most of it with the Orioles.

Sheets has wound up spending a lot of time at his new business. It's a multifaceted environment that's become very popular for birthday parties for children of all ages. His name helps draw people to the place at first, but then many come back if they love games and sports, and there's plenty of that there.

In addition, Sheets enjoys doing things like giving hitting lessons in an indoor baseball field and in batting cages that have grown very popular over the last few years. The indoor facility lets more baseball players work on their games during the fall and winter months so they can be ready for spring and summer competition.

One thing Sheets can show players is how to hit, because he did plenty of that with the Orioles. He probably didn't do quite as much as he wanted, but Sheets still helped the Orioles during his time with the team.

Sheets had shown he could hit with power during his first few years with the Orioles in the mid-1980s. But he wasn't able to get the guaranteed spot

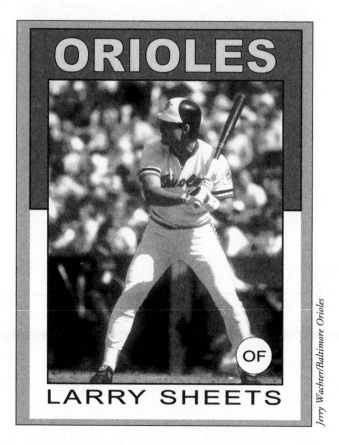

ORIOLES

OF

LARRY SHEETS

Jerry Wachter/Baltimore Orioles

#18 LARRY SHEETS • OF
Seasons with the Orioles: 1984-1989

Best Season with the Orioles: 1987
Highlight Stats from that Season: Sheets finished with career highs in homers (31), RBI (94), and average (.316). He finally got a regular spot in the lineup and found his stroke, becoming one of the most dangerous hitters on a Baltimore team that couldn't find its way all season long.

in the lineup that would give him the confidence and the ability to relax more.

Sheets hit a respectable 17 homers and had 50 RBI during his rookie year in 1985 and added 18 homers with 60 RBI in 1986. He batted .262 his first year and had a .272 average the second season. But he still couldn't get that regular lineup spot, because the Orioles were still relying heavily on the platoon system they'd used for many years.

However, everything changed in 1987 when then-manager Cal Ripken Sr. eventually pulled Sheets out of the platoon system that forced the left-handed hitter to the bench in certain situations. Sheets hit 10 homers in May and stayed hot for the rest of the season, finishing with a career-best 31 homers, 94 RBI, and a .316 batting average. Ripken let him play, and Sheets's confidence kept growing, and he finished with his best season ever.

"It was just one of those years when it all clicked," Sheets said. "I was no longer being platooned for the last third of the season... and it was always [then] when you walked in that door, you knew you were going to be in that lineup."

The interesting part of that season is Sheets didn't hit any homers in April. But he took off with the 10-homer month in May, even more impressive considering the fact that Sheets spent the season batting eighth or ninth. He'd usually bat eighth against right-handers and ninth versus left-handers, and he finished ninth in the American League with the .316 average.

"I would rather bat eighth or ninth [because] that 10th spot wasn't very good," Sheets said with a laugh.

Sheets said positive imaging was a big reason that he fared so well that season. He literally could see good hits coming before he came to bat. He just felt everything coming together and grew so confident that he became more aggressive at the plate and played a big role on an Orioles team that was one of the worst in the American League that season.

"Everything was so realistic to me," Sheets said. "I could be in the on-deck circle and visualize hitting the pitcher's best pitch. It was so realistic that I could hear the crack of the bat in my mind."

Sheets also said being in the lineup gave him a confidence that he hadn't been able to find before. Sheets said that Ripken told him, after the fast start, that he'd be playing every day because he'd earned that right. Not having to worry about when and if he'd be playing proved helpful.

In addition, Sheets got more time in the field and away from the designated hitter spot where he'd been throughout most of his first two seasons.

Sheets wound up playing right or left field and got away from the tough DH job, a role he had never loved.

"It's the hardest position in baseball," Sheets said. "There's no question about it."

But Sheets never could match his 1987 numbers again. He hit 10 homers with 47 RBI in 1988, and his average slid to .230. That season was bad for nearly everyone associated with the Orioles because the team set the major league record with 21 straight losses to start the season. Everything went wrong for the Orioles and Sheets. He couldn't find the power stroke of 1987, began pressing a little, and struggled most of the season.

He had problems again in 1989, finishing with just seven homers and 33 RBI in 102 games while batting just .243 as Baltimore rallied from its infamous 107-loss season to nearly win the American League East. The Orioles ran out of patience and traded him to Detroit. Sheets had 10 homers and 52 RBI with the Tigers in 1990, his final full season in the majors.

Why he couldn't find his 1987 form again remains a mystery to Sheets several years later. It's easy to hear in his voice. But now he doesn't have to worry about it. Now he just worries about teaching children to be the best hitters they can be and having fun at his place.

"You don't know what pushes the right buttons," Sheets said. "After [1987], I was never able to get that back for some reason. It was just something I was never able to get back and could never really figure out."

Sheets has also been working as the head baseball coach at the Gilman School, a private school in Baltimore, since 2010. One of his players was Ryan Ripken, Cal Ripken, Jr.'s son. Cal also has helped Sheets coach at Gilman.

FRANK ROBINSON

Not an Old 30

The line became a famous one in Baltimore baseball history. When the Orioles acquired Frank Robinson from Cincinnati in December 1965, then-general manager Bill DeWitt made a comment that would live for a long time.

DeWitt said that Robinson was "an old 30." That remark infuriated Robinson, and he went on to win the Triple Crown with the Orioles in 1966 and help the club capture its first world championship. Robinson became a true leader, the type of person the club needed to get over the top after coming close to winning the American League a few times.

Robinson had a Hall of Fame career as a player. He was with the Orioles for five successful seasons before the team traded him to Los Angeles in a multiplayer deal following the 1971 season. The Orioles still had lots of success after that trade—but never were quite the same.

But Robinson kept making news after that. He became the first African-American manager in baseball history in 1976 with Cleveland. Later he became a successful manager with San Francisco in the early 1980s and came back to help turn the Orioles around after a disastrous 107-loss season in 1988. That was the "Why Not?" season of 1989 when the Orioles were in the pennant race until the next-to-last day of the season—two painful losses in Toronto took them out of contention.

He then went to Montreal in 2002 and again did another strong turnaround job with a team worn thin by financial problems. Robinson then became the first manager of the Washington Nationals—and nearly turned that team into the surprise story of 2005. They were 50-31 at one point before fading. But they still stayed in the race until the very end.

ORIOLES

FRANK
ROBINSON
OF

#20 FRANK ROBINSON • OF
Seasons with the Orioles: 1966-1971

Best Season with the Orioles: 1966
Highlight Stats from that Season: He did everything that year, winning the American League Triple Crown by hitting .316 with 49 homers and 122 RBI to lead the Orioles to their first World Series title. The Hall of Famer blasted the game-winning homer in Game 4 of the Series with Los Angeles, which completed the surprising sweep.

Robinson was solid as a player throughout his career, but grew as a manager in each of his stints. He did a great job with the Orioles in the 1989 turnaround season, but he may have done his best work with the 2005 Nationals. In just their first year in the nation's capital, and with a low-budget team, Robinson masterfully put all of the pieces together to keep Washington in the race.

"We are not going to hang our heads about it, but we know our record should have been much better, and we'll try to do better next year," Robinson told reporters. "We were always trying to put someone out there who was hurt. When you do that, it just gets to you after a while. After they came back from their injuries, they were working their way back into the lineup and that caught up with us. There's nothing we can do about it. The harder we tried to right the ship, the worse it got."

The 81-81 record the Nationals finished with left Washington in fifth place in the very tough National League East, but it was the third time in his four years in charge of the franchise that Robinson's team had at least a .500 record or better. What made the task harder was the Nationals have one of the lowest payrolls in the sport.

Robinson was delighted at season's end, especially with the bolstering the Washington area gave the team, especially considering the District wasn't exactly known for being huge supporters of the sport.

"Probably, without [the fans], we wouldn't have the season we had," Robinson said to reporters. "They were an outstanding group of people, not only at the stadium, but out in the community. They were always pumping us up. We just played a terrible ballgame, and they would say, 'Don't worry about it. We are just happy to have you here.' I've never been connected to anything like that before."

Robinson had a 314-334 record through the four-year span and signed a one-year deal to return to Washington for the 2006 season.

"We are happy to have Frank back," Washington general manager Jim Bowden told MLB.com when Robinson signed the contract. "He kept the team competitive even though it had one of the lowest payrolls in the [NL East]."

Robinson did a good job of keeping a young Washington team on an even keel. The Nationals went up and down, but Robinson helped everyone stay calm. During one stretch early in the season, Robinson just smiled when asked if he was worried that the team was having some hitting problems and was slow to score runs.

"You have to have patience; that's the way this game is," Robinson said. "If you're playing football, you'd be in trouble right now. But you're not playing football, thank goodness."

Many wondered at first if Robinson would be a good manager. Those who lead teams must be good communicators and be able to deal with all types of players. In his younger days, Robinson was looked at as a bit of a troublemaker with the Cincinnati Reds, as a man who simply wasn't afraid to speak up for what he wanted. But he truly grew into a leader.

That's the key role he took when coming to Baltimore in 1966. The Orioles had plenty of talent; young pitching like Dave McNally, Jim Palmer, Wally Bunker, and Steve Barber and other players like Brooks Robinson, Paul Blair, Davey Johnson, and Boog Powell. But they needed one more piece to the puzzle. The Robinson trade involved giving up a solid pitcher in Milt Pappas, but the Orioles thought their new outfielder was worth the price.

Robinson had little trouble adjusting to the American League in 1966. He tore up the junior circuit, winning the rare and elusive Triple Crown by hitting .316 with 49 homers and 122 RBI. One of his best hits was a home run that left a lasting impression at Memorial Stadium. Robinson blasted a long homer off Cleveland's Luis Tiant on May 8 that flew out of the stadium through the left field bleachers.

The ball landed in the parking lot behind the bleachers. And the Orioles came up with a unique way to mark what Robinson did—putting up a flag that said simply, "Here," on the back end of the bleachers. Any self-respecting Orioles fan knew exactly what that meant.

But Robinson did more for the team than just hitting. He became a leader who did so much in the clubhouse. The Orioles eventually started the "Kangaroo Court" where after a win he doled out fines to players, little amounts for not doing some baseball things right. Robinson wore a mop on top of his head and the players would often chant, "Here comes the judge!" and the charges or violations would be announced. They would be for tiny things like not moving a runner up, overthrowing a cutoff man, and the like. But these things helped ensure the Orioles kept their eyes on the little parts of the game. And Robinson was the man who stuck with it.

He also had to come back from a frightening injury during the 1967 season after a collision while sliding to break up a double play left him with double vision that affected his hitting. But his sight corrected itself over time, and he and the Orioles got everything going for 1969. That's when they took off, winning the American League three straight years while posting 109, 108, and 101 victories. Robinson played a big role in helping the team make the World Series three straight times, even though they won just once.

One play Robinson made in the 10th inning of Game 6 of the 1971 World Series exemplified exactly what he was as a player. At 35 years old and slowing down a bit, Robinson still wasn't afraid to take a chance.

Pittsburgh held a three-games-to-two edge and was looking to close the Series out on a cool Saturday afternoon in Baltimore. The Orioles rallied from an early 2-0 deficit to tie and force the game into the 10th. Robinson drew a one-out walk, and Merv Rettenmund followed with a soft single to center. However, Robinson never stopped and went hard for third and just beat Vic Davalillo's throw. That proved to be a crucial play as Brooks Robinson followed with a sacrifice fly to medium center. If Frank Robinson hadn't taken that chance and gotten to third, there would have been no sacrifice fly.

The Orioles traded him after that season to Los Angeles in a blockbuster deal. Baltimore made the playoffs again in 1973 and 1974 and stayed competitive for several years after that, but many felt the Orioles weren't quite the same team again without a leader like Robinson.

Robinson gave the Orioles the kind of rare in-the-clubhouse leadership that's very hard to find. He truly was a lower-key Michael Jordan or a different version of Brett Favre. Orioles players routinely admitted that Robinson's leadership proved crucial to pushing them over the top and making Baltimore a feared and powerful team.

The big bat helped also, but Robinson's ability to make plays that showed how to play the game proved crucial. He did it so many times in so many ways. Robinson once made a catch where his back hit the wall so hard that he could barely swing the bat. But he didn't want to come out because the game was in extra innings. So what did he do at the plate minutes later? He shocked everyone and dropped a perfect bunt. That was typical Frank Robinson and why the Orioles missed him so much when he left.

Robinson was the manager when Montreal moved to Washington and became the Nationals, but the team let him go at the end of the 2006 season. After that, Robinson was honored with a statue at Oriole Park in 2012 and still worked as Major League Baseball's executive vice president of baseball development.

CURT MOTTON

Helping in a Pinch

C urt Motton was much like Terry Crowley during his days with the Orioles. Both were solid role players who turned out to be strong pinch hitters.

He's also like Crowley in that he returned to the Orioles, years after his baseball career ended. Motton worked in community affairs with the Orioles more than 30 years after his major league career ended.

Motton helped the Orioles with a variety of work in the community, in a semi-retired mode. He enjoyed doing things to help the team where he had his greatest moments on the baseball field. Motton had some coaching jobs in baseball, mostly with the Orioles, and he kept coming back to the team in different ways.

"I enjoy being [part of the Orioles]," Motton said.

However, Motton knew exactly what he meant to the team during his playing days. Simply put, Motton had no delusions of grandeur about his job with the team during its glory years.

The right-handed-hitting Motton knew that manager Earl Weaver would use him mostly as a pinch hitter as the Orioles had a powerful lineup that played on a regular basis. Motton eventually understood that, took pride in his job, and worked like crazy to be the best he could at it.

"There's always a challenge," Motton said. "Regardless of the situation, you have to be ready to play, and it was difficult because everybody wants to play every day. Once I accepted [the way] I was going to be used, I wanted to do it as well as I could."

Motton became a valuable tool for Weaver and the Orioles and came up with his two biggest pinch hits in playoff games. Motton's RBI single in the

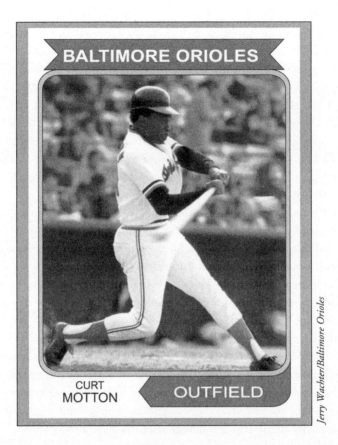

BALTIMORE ORIOLES

CURT
MOTTON

OUTFIELD

Jerry Wachter/Baltimore Orioles

#21 CURT MOTTON • OF
Seasons with the Orioles: 1967-1971, 1973-1974

Best Season with the Orioles: 1969
Highlight Stats from that Season: Motton did a lot of damage as a pinch
hitter that season. He finished with six homers and 21 RBI plus a .303
average in just 89 plate appearances. Manager Earl Weaver often used him
as a late-game pinch hitter, and he got the game-winning hit in Game 2 of
the ALCS against Minnesota, an 11th-inning single
that gave the Orioles a 1-0 win.

bottom of the 11th inning gave the Orioles a 1-0 victory over the Minnesota Twins in Game 2 of the 1969 American League Championship Series.

He came up with another huge pinch hit in Game 1 of the 1971 ALCS. Batting against Oakland's Vida Blue, Motton ripped a double down that left field line that tied the game, and the Orioles went on to a 5-3 victory. The Orioles swept both series—with Motton's hits proving to be clutch.

"I think people in Baltimore remember me because I was part of those [great] ball clubs," Motton said. "I had to be ready to do that. And that was the thing that kept me on my toes. I tried to stay in shape even though I wasn't playing."

There wasn't much mystery about Motton as a hitter. Now a part-time scout with the Orioles who also works in community relations, Motton was a dead-pull hitter who said he'd have probably been a good No. 6 or No. 7 hitter, but Weaver often batted him third, fourth, or fifth.

Weaver showed a lot of faith in Motton, repeatedly batting him in clutch situations. Motton knew he wasn't going to play every day and loved the challenge.

"Probably the thing that kept me keyed up and always ready was the way Earl used me," Motton said. "He almost always used me when it was a close ballgame. If I did my job, I was going to make a positive contribution to the ball club. The neat thing about my situation was that I was on such good ball clubs that we would get in games people would remember."

That's why many still remember what he did in the two ALCS games. The Orioles battled to pull out a 4-3 victory in Game 1 of the 1969 championship series and found themselves in another pitchers duel between Dave McNally and Baltimore native Dave Boswell the following day.

But the Orioles made some noise in the 11th inning when Boog Powell got to second base. Ron Perranoski came on in the 11th, but Motton singled to right field, scoring Powell to give the Orioles the key 1-0 win. They finished the sweep in Game 3.

"The pitch was away on the outer part of the plate, and I did something I rarely did—I hit it to right field," Motton said. "I just wanted to make good contact and hoped things would work out."

Motton did it again versus Blue in 1971. Blue was the talk of the baseball world in 1971 and shut down the Orioles for much of Game 1 of the ALCS as Oakland was in front. The Orioles had cut the A's lead to 3-2 before Motton lined a double to left that finally tied the game. Paul Blair then drove in the winning runs with a two-run double.

"It was a 3-1 count, and I was definitely looking fastball," Motton said. "I wouldn't have been upset if he had walked me. I would have taken a walk. Vida was unique. He had a fastball that was extremely difficult to catch up with. You could see it pretty good, but when it got close to home plate, it seemed like it picked up some velocity."

Interestingly, Motton got only one at-bat in the Orioles' three World Series appearances. He grounded out in the ninth inning of Game 5 in 1969 against the New York Mets—on the first pitch.

Motton played eight seasons in the major leagues, ending in 1974 before going into coaching. But when he looked back on his career, the highlights were easy to remember.

"Those two hits were certainly the best I ever got," Motton said. "I look back and would I have liked to play every day? Yes, but you know, if you're not going to be a regular, be on a good ball club. There's nothing like post-season, and there's nothing like a championship ball club."

Motton died in January, 2010, after having problems with cancer. He remained a popular figure among fans of the era in which he played.

JOHN STEFERO

A Few Big Hits

Many Orioles fans don't remember John Stefero. He's the quintessential example of a person who gets his 15 minutes of fame and then proceeds to get a whole lot of out of it.

The truth is his 15 minutes of fame came over about a two-day period about 22 years ago. But people who were Orioles fans and study team history still ask about him. And he loves talking about it.

Stefero didn't have a very long major league career. He played a total of 79 games over three seasons with the Orioles and later the then-Montreal Expos. But he gave Orioles fans two of their most dramatic and memorable moments during the 1983 world championship season by getting game-winning walkoff hits on consecutive days against the Milwaukee Brewers—the defending American League champions.

Those two hits during the final months of that season still make Stefero smile. And why shouldn't they? The situation was perfect for those who love baseball—a rookie backup catcher with little experience has to bat against a flame-throwing right-hander from a very good team.

Stefero was a left-handed hitter who singled off Milwaukee's Pete Ladd in the bottom of the ninth to give the Orioles a bizarre, come-from-behind 10-9 win on September 18. The rookie's hit wrapped up one of the biggest comebacks in team history, as the Brewers held a 7-0 lead at one point in the game.

Stefero liked it so much that he did it again the next day. He faced Tom Tellman and singled off of him in the bottom of the 11th inning to give the Orioles a 5-4 victory and cement his place in the annals of Orioles storytelling.

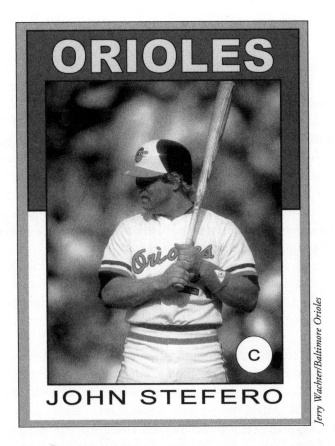

ORIOLES

JOHN STEFERO

Jerry Wachter/Baltimore Orioles

Best Season with the Orioles: 1986
Highlight Stats from that Season: This was his longest stretch in the major leagues. Stefero finally got some playing time,
hitting .233 in 52 games.

"It's something that you'll never forget for the rest of your life," Stefero said. "Anytime you do something like that, it's one of the highlights of your career. It's always something you'll remember."

Stefero remembers a lot of small, but funny things about that weekend. He remembers being forced to run from the left field bullpen at Memorial Stadium down to the team's third base dugout, quickly strip off his catching gear that he'd been using to warm up pitchers during the game, and grab a bat to get ready to hit in the ninth inning of the second game.

The first game was probably one of most memorable of Stefero's career. His major league debut had come earlier that season, but manager Joe Altobelli sent him in to run for Rick Dempsey when the catcher was hit by a pitch in the third inning. The Orioles were already trailing 7-0, as Milwaukee roughed up Orioles starter Jim Palmer.

The Orioles then slowly started to rally. Stefero walked in the fifth inning and then reached first on an error to lead off the seventh. He later scored as the O's cut the deficit to 7-3. Stefero kept his roll going in the eighth, singling and scoring as the Orioles rallied for six runs and took a 9-7 lead.

Milwaukee tied it in the ninth before Stefero and the Orioles locked things up in the bottom of the inning. Glenn Gulliver started the trouble with a one-out single to right, and Lenn Sakata followed with a walk. Stefero then singled to right for the game-winning hit.

"They knew he was a power pitcher, and I was a power hitter, so to speak," Stefero said. "I wasn't looking to hit a home run. I just wanted to make good, solid contact. At that point, you don't want to strike out, and you want to keep the momentum going."

He worried about the same thing the next day when coming to bat in the 11th inning—and came through once again. Stefero had come up earlier in the year when backup catcher Joe Nolan was hurt and got some brief action before returning back to the minors. The Orioles called him up again in September—having three catchers is a luxury teams don't often have with 25-man rosters—and he began having fun.

The second game saw Stefero pinch-hit again, this time in the ninth inning of a 7-7 tie with the winning run in scoring position. But Stefero lined out to left off of Tellman, and the game went to extra innings. But Stefero took care of things again, getting a game-ending single in the 11th off of Tellman to give the Orioles the win.

Stefero stayed on the team's active roster for the rest of the regular season as the Orioles wrapped up their second American League East crown in five years. He wasn't on the active roster for the playoffs, but remained in the bullpen and with the team during its victories in the American League Championship Series (over the White Sox) and the World Series (over the Phillies).

"Whether playing or not playing, it's a very nervous situation," Stefero said. "You're on national TV, and you don't want to make a mistake to make you look silly. Just to be there, the pregame ceremonies, the hoopla, it was well worth it."

Those days were the highlights of his career. Stefero had 11 at-bats during the 1983 season and didn't play for Baltimore again until 1986. He saw more playing time that season, appearing in 52 games and batting .233 with two homers and 13 RBI. That was the end of his Orioles career, however, because they sent Stefero to the Montreal Expos that winter as part of the Dennis Martinez trade. Stefero then batted .186 in 18 games with the Expos in 1987, but never made it back to the big leagues again, retiring about four years later after struggling with an elbow injury.

Stefero got into the car business after leaving baseball. He still lives in Baltimore and began working at Brown's selling cars. The former catcher found out that he enjoyed working with cars and made it his full-time job.

He also found a lot of success there, moving up the ladder and becoming general manager of the company. Stefero's been with the company for more than 20 years now—but still has a baseball itch at times.

He became a silent partner in Frozen Ropes, a baseball facility in the Glen Burnie area. Talking in 2004, Stefero wondered about maybe getting back into coaching some day. It's hard for him to walk away from a game he always played.

"You don't realize what you miss until it's gone, and baseball eventually goes away from all of us," Stefero said from his office at the car dealership. "I miss it severely. It's not the prestige; it's the other things that you miss. Baseball, and actually sports in general, is such a rewarding thing."

Especially those two days 31 years ago.

Stefero remains in the world of cars. He's the GM of Brown's Toyota, a dealership just outside of Baltimore.

Where Have You Gone?

JIM PALMER

The Classic Pitcher

J im Palmer was one of the best pitchers of his era. The tall, tanned right-hander had a classic delivery, with the high leg kick, and did so many things just right. He won his first World Series game as a 20-year-old start-er—beating the great Sandy Koufax—and his last at age 37, coming on in relief to give the Orioles a key win against the Phillies in Game 3 of the 1983 World Series. He overcame early arm troubles that threatened his career, had battles with manager Earl Weaver that made many giggle, and developed into one of the game's best clutch pitchers.

The right-hander finished with a career record of 268-162 and a 2.86 ERA, and was an easy first-ballot pick for the Hall of Fame in 1990. He almost always pitched well in clutch games, went 7-5 in postseason games, and won 20 games in a season eight times. In addition, Palmer captured the Cy Young Award three times—and, interestingly enough, never gave up a grand-slam homer.

Palmer became one of baseball's best-known pitchers. Even though he retired early in the 1984 season, Palmer is still respected by today's pitchers. The Hall of Famer has been a longtime television analyst for the Orioles and on national networks, and it's not uncommon to see pitchers on any team stop Palmer—who still looks like he's in playing shape—to talk pitch-ing. And he'll give information to anyone. He and Boston right-hander Curt Schilling spent several minutes talking about some of the intricacies of pitching in the clubhouse when the Red Sox first came to Baltimore during the 2005 season. In fact, it's almost a regular happening.

Palmer also has a fabulous memory, something that helped him during his playing days and aids him now during his TV broadcasts. He can re-

88

#22 JIM PALMER • P
Seasons with the Orioles: 1965-1967, 1969-1984

Best Season with the Orioles: 1975
Highlight Stats from that Season: The Hall of Famer was the Cy Young winner with some impressive numbers. He finished 23-11 with 25 complete games and 10 shutouts along with a 2.09 ERA. Palmer led the league in wins, shutouts, and ERA; threw a career-best 323 innings; and made the All-Star Game.

member the pitch he threw to a player in 1971, the count, and what happened—and will make fun of himself about what should have happened if it wasn't a good finish. It's easy to see that Palmer likes doing TV broadcasts because that allows him to stay close to baseball.

"I enjoy coming to the ballpark because you always learn something more about the game or life or somebody's different perspective about somebody and the way they feel about something," Palmer said. "It's a constant learning situation… and I enjoy broadcasting, and I try to be prepared, and it's very much like playing—other than there's not a physical part of it."

Broadcasting was one of the things that helped Palmer become one of the better nationally known pitchers of his era. He began working on TV while still an active player, working with broadcasters like Howard Cosell, and was a natural right away. Palmer now has been broadcasting in some form since the mid-1970s and takes pride in his work.

"You want to be prepared, and you want to be part of a team," Palmer said. "You have to work with that guy you're working with."

He also became rather well known and very popular, especially with female fans and non-fans alike, for his Jockey underwear advertisements. The combination of the ads, the clutch pitching, the 20-win seasons, and the TV broadcasting has made Palmer arguably the best-known pitcher of his time.

Palmer signed with the Orioles in 1963 and said he's still grateful that he made that tough decision.

"My best thing was just signing with the Orioles," Palmer said. "When you're 17 years old, you don't know where you're going to end up or what you're going to do. [It's tough]. But it turned out great. You think back on your career and you wonder where you could have ended up. I could have ended up with the Dodgers or Houston or whatever. I… made the right decision."

It certainly looks that way. Palmer gained national acclaim when the Orioles pulled off their surprising run to the 1966 World Series. The 20-year-old right-hander had a 15-10 record with a 3.46 ERA and found himself facing Sandy Koufax in Game 2 of the World Series in Los Angeles. Baltimore had shocked the baseball world in Game 1 by beating the Dodgers, using a big relief effort from Moe Drabowsky, and Los Angeles didn't want to go back to Baltimore trailing two games to none.

But Palmer showed the poise and cool of a veteran and pitched a complete game, a 6-0 shutout of the Dodgers—who were hurt badly by out-

fielder Willie Davis's three errors. The Orioles went on to sweep the World Series, and Koufax retired after the Series, citing bad elbow problems.

Palmer's career seemed about to take off, and the Orioles seemed ready to become a dynasty. But everything went wrong after that for the young player and his team. Palmer began to have arm problems in 1967, difficulties that slowed him down for about two years. Many wondered if his career was over, but Palmer made it back when the Orioles destroyed the American League in 1969. Palmer had to go on the disabled list during the season, but rebounded later with a no-hitter against Oakland, finishing with a 16-4 record.

That was the beginning for Palmer, who quickly began to show a penchant for winning clutch games. He won Game 3 of the 1969 American League Championship Series to clinch the title and sent the Orioles to the World Series for their ill-fated meeting with the New York Mets. After that, he won the ALCS clincher in 1970 and 1971. Palmer—who had the nickname "Cakes" for his love of pancakes—also won three World Series games for the powerful Orioles and earned a reputation as one of the game's best clutch pitchers.

Palmer also was known for his battles with manager Earl Weaver. Both men had little trouble speaking their minds and often did it to—and about—each other. That's even continued in some ways now years after both have retired. The two combined on a book project a few years ago, and then Weaver fired some blistering shots at Palmer during a banquet both were at.

But both shook that off, saying it's par for the course for their relationship. No matter what they say about each other, the respect that's there isn't hard to see.

"Earl and I had our love-hate relationship, but at the end of the day, he always gave me the responsibility to win or lose games," Palmer said. "We both ended up in the Hall of Fame, and we were both part of some very special opportunities and things that happened here in Baltimore."

Palmer appreciated the fact that Weaver consistently gave him the ball in big games and saw him as the pitcher the Orioles needed. Many of the games Palmer pitched were the crucial ones, games the team couldn't afford to lose.

"He trusted me, and he trusted that I could pitch late in the ballgame," Palmer said. "He may have aggravated me, but he certainly made me a better pitcher."

One of Palmer's best years came in 1971, the season the Orioles won their third straight American League East title and American League championship. The Orioles eventually wasted a two games-to-none lead over Pittsburgh in the World Series, losing in seven games. But Palmer won Game 2 and turned in a strong effort in Game 6, when the Orioles needed to win to stay alive in the Series.

But the 1971 Orioles did something that probably won't ever happen again. They compiled one of the best pitching staffs ever when Palmer, Mike Cuellar, Dave McNally, and Pat Dobson, whom Baltimore acquired in a trade before the season, all became 20-game winners.

Palmer actually became the last of the quartet to reach the 20-win plateau, getting it on the final day of the season. Being part of that is something he's still proud of.

"It was a different era; it was a different environment," Palmer said. "It was a very special time. I was the last guy to do it... and you always felt pressure to pitch well for the ball club. All I had to do was be healthy, and I was going to have success because we had such a great team."

Palmer, involved with the Orioles as an analyst on many of their TV broadcasts, was one of the players the Orioles honored with a statue at Oriole Park during the 2012 season.

Where Have You Gone?

CHRIS HOILES

Truly a Good Catch

W hen his major league career ended, former Orioles catcher Chris
Hoiles proved that you really can go home again.

Hoiles retired in 1999 after being slowed by back and hip problems. He
was 34 years old when the Orioles let him go just before that season began
mainly due to those health issues. But Hoiles slowly worked his way back
into coaching and joined Bowling Green as a volunteer assistant coach,
working there for three years and enjoying his time. Hoiles was from the
area near the Ohio school and got to work back in baseball again as well as
got a chance to watch his three little boys grow up.

"It's a great age group," Hoiles said late in 2004. "It's a great age to work
with, and I've enjoyed [my time]. The kids, they're still wanting to learn,
and it's been good."

But things got even better for Hoiles a few months later when he accept-
ed an official position as the assistant coach with his alma mater, Eastern
Michigan. He's one of the best-known players in school history, playing on
the team for three years before getting picked by Detroit in the 1986 draft.
The Tigers traded him to Baltimore midway through 1988 in the Fred
Lynn trade, and Hoiles never left Charm City.

Hoiles was a very low-key person when playing for the Orioles. He almost had to prove himself on a regular basis, not being the flashiest catcher
or having the greatest arm. But Hoiles was very consistent and stayed with
the Orioles for parts of 10 years, getting regular time behind the plate for
eight seasons.

Despite his quiet nature, the fans noticed him, picking Hoiles to the
Orioles' 50th anniversary team in 2004. Back at Oriole Park at Camden

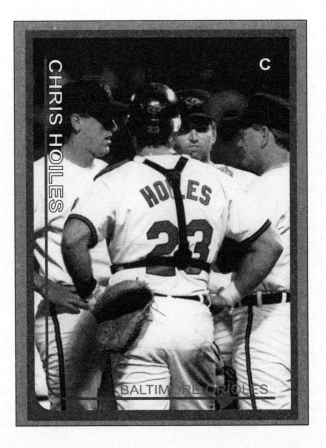

CHRIS HOILES

C

HOILES 23

BALTIMORE ORIOLES

#23 CHRIS HOILES • C
Seasons with the Orioles: 1989-1998

Best Season with the Orioles: 1993
Highlight Stats from that Season: Hoiles came through with career bests in homers (29) and RBI (82) to play a big role for the Orioles that season and even gain several votes in the American League MVP poll. He finished with a career-high .310 average and often sparked the Orioles offense.

Yards for the ceremony, Hoiles seemed very relaxed and happy with where he was at in his life. He still follows baseball constantly and might be doing more of that now that he's gotten back into coaching and hoping that could take him somewhere in the sport.

When asked if he missed the game, Hoiles's answer was a bit surprising. He was known for being a quiet individual when playing with the Orioles, not much of a talker. He simply did his job and moved on.

But the answer came without hesitation.

"Terribly," he said with a kind of bittersweet smile. "That's another outlet when you go through something like what I'm doing collegiately. You're able to pass it on, stay in the game, even though you can't play. There's always an aspect of the game of baseball that's [interesting]. I played it, I'm coaching it, and now I'm teaching it, and it's been a lot of fun."

He didn't have much fun toward the end of his career as hip and back problems slowed him greatly and caused him a lot of pain. Hoiles eventually had a hip replacement operation and was very glad to finally get it done—because his life is much more enjoyable.

"It's much better," Hoiles said. "It's great. It had gotten to the point where I had to do it. I could hardly walk anymore. I wish I had done it sooner."

He did some different things before getting back into coaching. Hoiles was involved with car racing before baseball called him once more. But he's certainly glad to be back with the sport he loved. That showed when Hoiles was talking about his career at the 50th anniversary celebration.

Hoiles looked around an extra clubhouse the Orioles have at Camden Yards and said what a great place that building was for him, especially because he always had to prove wrong those who thought he wasn't good enough to be a regular catcher.

"There's so many memories for me," Hoiles said. "Just making it to this level and being able to stick at this level. I think that everybody kind of has his doubters at some point in time, but with me I probably had more than my fair share. I think that if I look back at the career that I had, I think I can say I had some pretty good years."

Hoiles said he was fortunate to have so many good memories from his playing days in Baltimore. He saw Cal Ripken Jr. tie and then break Lou Gehrig's record for consecutive games played. He watched Eddie Murray return to the Orioles after a long time away and hit his 500th home run. On a personal note late in his career, Hoiles hit two grand slams against Cleveland (which was basically his hometown team) on August 14, 1998,

in a 15-3 Orioles win. He blasted a shot off Charles Nagy in the third and another off Ron Villone in the eighth.

A funny moment came when Hoiles, an Ohio native, actually got a standing ovation from the Cleveland fans in that game. He had several friends at the game and joked to reporters afterward, "I didn't know quite what to make of that. I don't know if they became O's fans for a minute or what."

Hoiles never made the All-Star Game but was a solid hitter for Baltimore, blasting over 20 home runs three times. His best year was in 1993 when Hoiles hit 29 homers and had 82 RBI in 126 games to earn Most Valuable Oriole honors. In addition, Hoiles posted a career-best .310 average and finished 16th in the American League in that year's Most Valuable Player voting.

Overall, he finished with 151 homers and 449 RBI in 894 games in his career, all of it with the Orioles, and Hoiles gained plenty of knowledge he likes to pass on as a coach. While volunteering at Bowling Green, Hoiles worked mostly with the catchers and hitters, teaching them about the game.

"The biggest thing I can pass on to the players is the knowledge I gained having played at the major league level," Hoiles said in an August 2001 article in the Bowling Green *Sentinel-Tribune*. "It'll be a lot of fun to pass that knowledge on to other players to help them improve. I've also played with a number of big-name players, and even though I didn't follow their style or what they were doing, I can still pass on how they did things."

Hoiles certainly enjoyed his playing days at Eastern Michigan. He set school records for single-season RBI (70 in 1986) and homers (19 also in 1986) along with career homers (34). Hoiles also posted very high batting averages during his three years (.340, .372, and .342) and finished with a career mark of .352. The school retired his No. 32 jersey—could that explain why he wore 23 with the Orioles?—in 1994 and inducted him into the EMU Athletics Hall of Fame six years later.

But Hoiles certainly doesn't mind being back in college once more. He's back in baseball, working on coaching, maybe moving higher on that ladder, and getting a chance to watch his three young boys grow up near where he grew up. And they're starting to play baseball, too.

Can it get any better than that?

Hoiles did a number of things in recent years involving baseball. He coached at different levels, managed the York Revolution, helped the Orioles in Spring Training, and has said he'd love to get some kind of bigger job with his former team, since they've already made positions for other ex-Birds.

Where Have You Gone?

RICK DEMPSEY

The Dipper

Rick Dempsey is known for so many things to Baltimore Orioles fans. Catchers are often considered to be much like goalies in other sports—not always wrapped too tightly—and Dempsey has lived up to that notion several times.

There was the now-famous time when the Orioles were playing in Boston, and a strong rainstorm delayed the game. Dempsey then put a bunch of stuff under his jersey, pretended to be Babe Ruth, and crossed over a bit by acting out Carlton Fisk's homer in the 1975 World Series. Then he ran around the bases and ended the bit by sliding belly-first across the plate. The act drew a huge ovation from those of the Red Sox Nation watching and made Dempsey famous in certain ways.

Fans always wanted him to do that stunt—something that's still replayed on television more than 25 years later. But Dempsey should have been known for what he really was, which was a very good defensive catcher who knew how to call a game and handle a pitching staff. He was one of few to play in four decades—from 1969 to 1992 and despite having just a .233 career batting average, showed a real ability to get clutch hits at clutch times.

Dempsey has remained in baseball in various ways since his career ended in 1992. He's been a coach, a minor league manager, a television commentator, and most recently a coach with the Orioles. He served as first base coach and then moved to third base when Sam Perlozzo took over as interim manager in August 2005. But the Orioles then moved him to the bullpen for 2006, a move he reportedly wasn't ecstatic with. However, he agreed to do it.

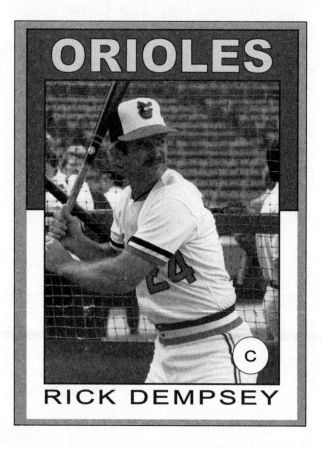

ORIOLES

RICK DEMPSEY

C

#24 RICK DEMPSEY • C
Seasons with the Orioles: 1976-1986, 1992

Best Season with the Orioles: 1985
Highlight Stats from that Season: The catcher hit 12 homers and drove in 52 RBI that season, along with a .254 average. It was Dempsey's best all-around season at the plate while with the Orioles.

Dempsey played in the 1979 and 1983 World Series with the Orioles and then caught for Los Angeles in the 1988 Series. The Dodgers pulled a huge upset in 1988, beating heavily favored Oakland four games to one, with Dempsey appearing in two games. However, Dempsey's greatest moments came in the 1983 Series when the Orioles beat Philadelphia in five games. He came up with several big hits as Baltimore bounced back after losing the first game to win four straight and capture its first world championship since 1970.

But Dempsey still deflects talk about himself winning the MVP award from that Series. He made the cover of *Sports Illustrated* the following week, but still makes the point that it was a team title that year.

"That was fun for me, and it was the culmination of a lot of things," Dempsey said. "If the team didn't play as well as it did, if Cal Ripken hadn't been the MVP of the league that year, and if all these guys hadn't pitched well, I'd have never gotten that opportunity."

Dempsey still insists his numbers weren't that staggering—he batted .385 with five hits total—but those hits were big. He had four doubles and a homer as the catcher came up with key hits at key times to help the Orioles scratch out four wins against a stubborn Philadelphia team.

"It wasn't that I had such a good World Series, because I was only five for 13," Dempsey said. "Robin Yount and Paul Molitor both had five hits in the first game of the World Series they played in versus the St. Louis Cardinals, and they lost. [My hits] just came at the right time, and it was just one of those things. I'll tell you what—it really should not have been Rick Dempsey the MVP, because Scotty McGregor had two great starts. Even though he lost 2-1 in the first one, he won the second one 5-0.

"Tippy Martinez had an outstanding Series. Everybody played well defensively, and the pitching was really the strength. Sammy Stewart just had a great Series, and everyone did well."

Interestingly enough, Dempsey's hitting was the last thing the Orioles needed from him. They wanted Dempsey more for his defensive plusses than anything else. This team had plenty of hitting and plenty of everything else during his career with the Orioles. But Dempsey knew how important the pitching was to the success of this team.

"Pitching was always first, and we protected our pitchers with great defense," Dempsey said. "Alongside that great defense, which filters down to your offense, we had enough guys in the lineup to hit the ball out of

the ballpark. Earl wanted that sort of offensive ball club, and we could put some runs up on the board. We had all the pieces put together back then."

Dempsey moved on to play with the Indians, Dodgers, and Brewers when he became a free agent following the 1986 season. He wound up with a similar role in Los Angeles and helped the Dodgers shock Oakland in the 1988 World Series. He's been trying to become a major league manager since retiring as a player but keeps coming up short. However, he'll keep on trying.

Dempsey, who often lived in California in the offseasons, also had plenty of baseball in his family life. The older of his two sons, John, caught in the St. Louis farm system. In addition, Rick's brother, Pat, caught in the minors for a number of teams, including the Orioles. And Rick's nephew, Gregg Zaun, developed into a solid big league catcher.

Zaun caught for the Orioles for parts of two seasons (1994, 1995) and has been with nine teams overall.

Dempsey has been with the Orioles TV network in recent years, usually serving as an analyst on pre- and post-game shows. Still a popular figure in the area, Dempsey opened a restaurant at Oriole Park and sings with a local band.

Where Have You Gone?

DAVE SCHMIDT

Trying to Make More Good Pitchers

Dave Schmidt was a solid major league pitcher. He could work as both
a starter and a reliever and had a 3.88 ERA over a 12-year career in
the majors.

Now he's taking the knowledge he learned over all of those years and
games and helping pitchers who want to make it to the majors. Schmidt
worked in the Orioles' farm system for several years. Schmidt had his greatest success with the Orioles, twice winning 10 games (a career best), and he
came back to the team after his playing career ended.

Schmidt loves working with young pitchers. He's handled various jobs
in the Orioles system, including being the pitching coach with two other
minor league teams and serving as the team's minor league pitching coordinator for three years. He loves working with up-and-coming pitchers.

"Working with kids kind of keeps me young," Schmidt said. "I have a
son; he's 21 this year. It kind of keeps me current with my own kids a little
bit. But I enjoy working with [the IronBirds pitchers] and seeing them
improve. If you can establish a foundation of some respect and trust with
those kids, they'll do a lot."

Schmidt's worked with a lot of young kids in the Orioles system, because the team has spent time trying hard to find more good arms. Schmidt
enjoys playing his role.

"They'll really work hard for you," Schmidt said. "But you really have
to work hard to get that [respect]."

Schmidt said one thing that helps him get that respect is the fact that
they know he pitched in the major leagues. But interestingly enough, the

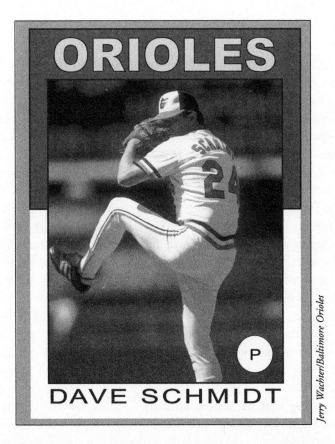

ORIOLES

DAVE SCHMIDT

P

Jerry Wachter/Baltimore Orioles

Best Season with the Orioles: 1988
Highlight Stats from that Season: Schmidt had nearly identical years in
1987 (10-5) and 1988 (8-5), but to be a winning pitcher in the latter season truly was an accomplishment. The reason—the Orioles lost their first
21 games and 107 overall. But Schmidt pitched nicely throughout. He
pitched in 41 games, starting nine, and tossed 129⅔ innings
with an impressive 3.40 ERA.

game that stands out the most in Schmidt's Orioles career is one that, under most situations, would have meant very little to anyone.

The Orioles were already far out of the pennant race when they took the field on April 29, 1988. They had lost their first 21 games and had the baseball world—along with most everyone else—laughing. The Orioles were already the butt of jokes on late-night shows and just about everywhere else. They already had fired one manager—Cal Ripken Sr. after just six games—and were headed for a very long year.

Bill Ripken had been featured on the cover of *Sports Illustrated* in a rather somber pose during the latter parts of the losing streak, and players were facing questions from a growing media group nearly every night. Frank Robinson took over after Cal Ripken Sr. was let go and was working hard at trying to turn things around, but nothing had been working.

"The streak was kind of crazy, because I don't think there were too many games where we actually were blown out," Schmidt said. "There were a lot of close games where strange things happened at the end of the game to us, an error or a crazy play. We were getting beat in every conceivable way during the streak, and so the night we finally won, there was some pressure, because you get to the point where you've lost 21 in a row, you're almost sitting around and waiting to see what's going to happen for us tonight to lose."

Something kept happening until the Orioles met the Chicago White Sox at Comiskey Park on April 29. The night before that game, Robinson pulled aside Schmidt and Mark Williamson and gave them a message. The skipper told the pair that Williamson would start and go the first six innings when they got to Chicago, and Schmidt would close out the final three, and they'd stop the streak.

And that's just what happened.

Everything finally turned around on that cool Friday night in Chicago. Williamson, whose best career work came later as a setup man, started occasionally for the Orioles in the early days of his career. He turned in a solid effort that night, giving up three hits and striking out two in six shutout innings. Schmidt then came in and slammed the door, allowing only one hit over the final three innings as Baltimore locked up a 9-0 victory.

Everything finally went right in this game. Cal Ripken singled, and Eddie Murray followed by hitting a two-run homer in the top of the first inning to give the Orioles a lead they never lost. The lead kept growing, and everyone kept hoping that this was the night the streak would end. And it finally did.

"We just needed to get over that hump and get rid of that feeling," Schmidt said.

The right-handed starter/reliever said the players were just so glad to get the media folks out of the clubhouse and stop having to answer questions about the losing streak. (The Orioles nearly went the entire month of April without a win.) Those were questions that they were sick of answering—although many gave Robinson credit for keeping everyone focused and loose during that time.

Schmidt was one of the few pitchers who actually found success that season. He tied for the most wins on the team (eight) and was the only pitcher with a winning record (8-5). Schmidt appeared in 41 games, starting nine, and had an impressive 3.40 ERA. He pitched in 129⅔ innings, the second-most of his career.

Many had suspected the Orioles would struggle again after having lost 95 in 1987, the first year after manager Earl Weaver's second and final retirement, but no one expected such a horrifying start. The team finished 54-107, and people didn't expect much from them in 1989. However, the Orioles surprised people again by coming up with one of the best turnarounds in baseball history.

Baltimore challenged for first place throughout 1989, leading for a long stretch and shocking everyone with an 87-75 record. The Orioles were in the battle until the final weekend of the season where they lost two painful games to Toronto, letting the Blue Jays clinch the division. But Schmidt said that 1989 was a joy overall, especially after battling through 1988.

"Hey, 1989 was a fun year," Schmidt said. "We had a lot of young players who had a lot of energy. [Jeff] Ballard, [Gregg] Olson, guys just had great years. We played great defense, and we got key hits and our young starters performed well. We surprised everybody; we snuck up on so many teams. We surprised ourselves a little bit, but once we got it going, the confidence sort of built."

Schmidt finished the season with a 10-13 record in his only season where he really spent most of the time as a starter. He started a career-high 26 games and threw a career-best 156⅔ innings. However, he also finished with a career-worst 5.69 ERA despite pitching very well for long stretches for a team that just wouldn't quit. Schmidt's pitching played a big role in helping the team that season.

"Instead of sitting there wondering how we're going to lose this game, we're sitting there every night figuring, 'Well, we're going to win somehow,'" Schmidt said. "It was just the reverse of the previous year."

Schmidt then left the Orioles after his third season (1989) and went to Montreal, and his career ended after a few appearances with Seattle in 1992. He officially retired in 1993 and kind of relaxed that summer before his old college coach from UCLA called and asked if he'd want to come and help coach the Bruins. Schmidt liked the idea and began helping out as a volunteer at UCLA before officially becoming the pitching coach for two more years. Schmidt then decided to go into professional coaching and has served his long stretch with the Orioles.

Schmidt said he's learned that there's no easy formula for being a pitching coach with kids much younger except to work hard and try to help everyone equally. He truly enjoys coaching and working with the players. He sat in his office at Ripken Stadium in Aberdeen late in the 2005 season and talked about how he's grown into the job and enjoys it.

"They know I played some major league baseball, but that respect, as far as baseball knowledge, will last about three minutes if I didn't show them that I know how to teach and [know] the game," Schmidt said. "You have to show them that you can teach, that you know what's going on, what will work, and what won't work."

Schmidt remained with the Orioles organization in a coaching role. He served as the Florida and Latin America Pitching Administrator in 2013— his 16th season with the franchise.

DAVE DUNCAN

A Good Catch

D ave Duncan always knew good pitching. He's seen a whole lot of it in more than 40 years of professional baseball. He's caught the best—like Jim Palmer and Catfish Hunter—and coached the best—like Dennis Eckersley and Dave Stewart—during his career as a catcher and later as a very well-respected pitching coach.

Duncan played for the Orioles during the final two years of his playing career in 1975 and 1976. He caught Palmer during back-to-back Cy Young Award seasons. Duncan also caught Wayne Garland during his surprise 20-win season in 1975.

However, Duncan spent many of his playing days in Oakland with an A's team that was growing by the minute. He had brief looks with the team in 1964 and 1967 while the franchise played in Kansas City and then got into the majors for good when the A's were just starting to blossom in 1968.

Duncan played with the A's until 1972 and was part of the team's first World Series win. Oakland then went on to win in 1973 and 1974, but Duncan spent those years with Cleveland before coming to Baltimore for the last two years of his career.

In an interview a few years ago, Duncan said he liked coming to Baltimore because he knew just how good the Orioles were at that time.

"The Orioles always played hard," Duncan said. "It was great to see Jim Palmer win the Cy Young Award both years I was in Baltimore, and Wayne Garland winning 20 games [was great]."

Garland had been a prospect the team liked before 1976, but he had a break-out season that year, going 20-7. The right-hander then left for

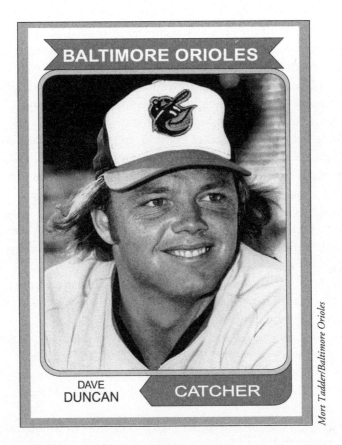

BALTIMORE ORIOLES

DAVE
DUNCAN   CATCHER

Mort Tadder/Baltimore Orioles

#25 DAVE DUNCAN • C
Seasons with the Orioles: 1975-1976

Best Season with the Orioles: 1975
Highlight Stats from that Season: Duncan batted only .205 but gave the
Orioles some punch with 12 homers and 41 RBI, despite playing only 96
games. He also did a fine job working with the
Orioles pitching staff that year.

Cleveland as one of the early free agents but stumbled. He went 13-19 the following season and never won more than six games in a season again.

But Duncan helped the Orioles for both seasons he was in Baltimore. Duncan played 96 games in 1975 with Baltimore and batted .205 with 12 homers and 41 RBI. He then hit .204 with four homers and 17 RBI the next year in 93 games. Duncan was well known as a solid defensive catcher who had some power but lacked the skills to be a good average hitter.

Duncan enjoyed playing with Baltimore as the team finished second in the tough American League East Division both seasons. The Orioles battled Boston for much of 1975 before taking second place and came up short in 1976 to the New York Yankees.

Duncan said in the interview that he enjoyed watching manager Earl Weaver because things weren't ever boring with him in the dugout during a game.

"Playing for Earl, you knew he was going to be in every game," Duncan said. "You never knew when the funniest thing you've ever seen was going to happen between him and an umpire."

Duncan had a career average of .214 but was especially known for his strong defensive work with Oakland, Cleveland, and the Orioles. The A's had lots of talented young pitchers when Duncan was there, namely Hunter, Vida Blue, Blue Moon Odom, and others, and he helped them grow into stronger veterans.

However, Duncan had some bad breaks, the worst of which came during the 1972 World Series, when Oakland made its first splash on the national stage. Gene Tenace had been Duncan's backup for much of the season, hitting just five homers in 82 games. But he had a regular role in Oakland's dramatic five-game win over Detroit in the American League Championship Series, and manager Dick Williams kept him there in the World Series.

Tenace homered on his first two at-bats in Game 1 and kept on going, getting four homers and playing a big role in Oakland's mildly surprising seven-game win. Duncan saw much of it from the bench, not even making an appearance until pinch-hitting in the bottom of the ninth of Game 5. He singled but was forced out as Cincinnati scored a 5-4 win.

Interestingly, Williams got both Tenace and Duncan in Game 7. Tenace played first base while Duncan caught as the A's took the championship with a 3-2 victory.

"He was a good defensive catcher," said former Oriole Don Buford. "He ranks as one of the good catchers. He was good all the way through."

Duncan was one of the unsung heroes of that first Oakland title team, which broke through to the World Series after losing to the Orioles in three straight in the 1971 ALCS. He was strong at handling the young and talented staff.

"He controlled their pitching all the way through and called good games," Buford said.

Duncan then went on to become a very successful pitching coach in the majors. He spent much of his time under manager Tony La Russa with the White Sox, A's, and Cardinals.

He found plenty of success at all of his stops, starting with Cleveland and then Seattle before catching up with La Russa in Chicago in 1983. The White Sox won the American League West that year before losing to the Orioles in the ALCS. He moved to Oakland in July 1986 and turned the A's into one of the best pitching staffs in the majors. They led the American League in ERA from 1988 through 1990.

He stayed with Oakland until the 1996 season when he moved to St. Louis with La Russa. Chris Carpenter won the Cy Young Award in 2005, the fourth Duncan pitcher to do so—Bob Welch, Eckersley, and LaMarr Hoyt were the others.

Duncan and his wife, Jeanine, have two sons, Christopher (drafted by the Cardinals as a supplemental first-round pick in the June 1999 amateur draft) and David (drafted by the New York Yankees in June 2001 draft), and make their offseason home in Jupiter, Florida.

Duncan remained one of the most respected pitching coaches in the major leagues while with the Cardinals. He stepped down from his job before the 2012 season to help his wife deal with her health problems.

Where Have You Gone?

DAVE JOHNSON

A Pitcher Who Remained Part of the Family

N ot many people had heard of Dave Johnson when he made his first
start with the Orioles during the "Why Not?" season of 1989. He
was helping a rotation that had been struggling as Baltimore tried to stay
close with Toronto for first place in the American League East one year
after losing an embarrassing 107 games.

Johnson was a hometown boy who made it on his favorite team. He
threw several good games down the stretch for the Orioles that season, but
then struggled while losing five straight. The Orioles were in Toronto in
need of a win in the second game of a three-game stint to stay alive in the
pennant race—a loss would eliminate Baltimore, because the team was two
games back with only two games left. Pete Harnisch was supposed to start
that day, but suffered an unusual injury, stepping on a nail while walking
in Toronto.

Johnson was called upon at the last minute and gave a heroic effort,
leaving in the eighth holding a two-run lead. But the Orioles bullpen fell
apart that inning, and Toronto rallied for a 4-3 win to clinch the division
title. Johnson became one of Baltimore's best pitchers in 1990, winning 13
games, but faded after that. However, many Orioles fans remember that
one big game, and Johnson stayed in baseball and with Baltimore over the
years.

His son, Steve Johnson, became the first player to be named to *The
Sun*'s All-Metro team four times. The six-foot-one, 195-pound Johnson
helped the Crusaders to a pair of Maryland Interscholastic Athletic As-
sociation A Conference titles and ended with a spectacular senior season.
Even though St. Paul's School didn't win the title his senior year in 2005,

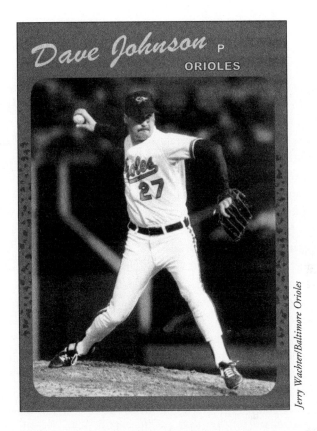

Dave Johnson P
ORIOLES

Jerry Wachter/Baltimore Orioles

#27 DAVE JOHNSON • P
Seasons with the Orioles: 1989-1991

Best Season with the Orioles: 1990
Highlight Stats from that Season: It was a career best for Johnson, helping his hometown team with a 13-9 record and a 4.10 ERA. The right-hander gave up 30 homers, but pitched consistently in 29 starts.

Johnson won 10 games, threw 93 innings, struck out 130 while walking only 15, and had a 1.27 ERA.

That was a big reason the Los Angeles Dodgers picked Johnson in the 13th round of the draft. Johnson finished with a 34-6 career record and went on to the Los Angeles farm system, something his father is very proud of.

He made the Orioles for stretches in 2012 and 2013 and battled injuries, but got chances to pitch both out of the bullpen and as a starter.

The elder Johnson also has done a lot of work with the Orioles TV broadcasts, usually as a studio analyst. He also has done a lot of community work and public relations for the team, something that helps him stay involved with baseball. He has run a baseball league for underprivileged kids in the Baltimore area for the Orioles.

Johnson's professional career taught him many tough lessons that he could pass on to his son and other children with whom he works. He's especially knowledgeable about pitchers and how they need to behave on the mound.

"My biggest thing I have stressed to [my son and other pitchers] was that you're going to have bad days, but you have to handle it properly," Johnson said. "When you're out on the mound, you can't act like a prima donna. You can't act like you're better than everyone. You have to be confident... in what you're going to do and that you're going to have days when things just don't go well. It's how you handle that that people are going to remember."

Johnson wants to get that message through to the kids he works with, especially in the me-first age that we live in today. He truly wants kids to remember that behaving like a good person is just as important as how well someone can play the game.

"I think that's not stressed enough in all sports," Johnson said. "You battle and you scratch and you claw and you do everything you can to win, but in the end, when the game's over, when the fight's over, the battle's over. Now it's time to just congratulate each other for doing the best you can and go get them the next time."

Johnson used that attitude throughout a long minor league career and finally made it to the majors in 1987 at the age of 27. He got in five games without a decision with Pittsburgh that year. Johnson became a free agent after 1988 and signed with Houston, who traded him to Baltimore late in spring training the following season.

He came up to the Orioles in the second half of the season and pitched surprisingly well. Johnson went 4-7, but had a respectable 4.23 ERA and tied for the club lead with four complete games despite making only 14 starts. He started 4-2, but lost five in a row, still not pitching badly. Johnson didn't always get a huge amount of run support from a Baltimore offense that was inconsistent at times.

But the Orioles had to call on him in the second game of the aforementioned Toronto series after Harnisch's strange injury. Johnson didn't know what was happening until he got to the ballpark in Toronto and found a ball in his locker, which the team gave to its daily starter. Johnson thought it was a mistake until discovering the true story.

He also didn't have a whole lot of time to get nervous. Johnson simply focused on trying to pitch the best he could.

"There was a lot of pressure, of course, but once the game starts, you don't feel that pressure. You really don't," Johnson said. "When you're a professional athlete and probably even into amateur baseball at the collegiate level and things like that, the game starts and there's no time to think about all those things that go into your mind before the game starts."

Johnson struggled a little in the first inning as Toronto scratched out a run on a walk, a ground out, and a single for a quick 1-0 lead. But the right-hander settled down after that and got into a groove.

"Once the game starts, it's what pitch am I going to throw, where am I going, what base am I backing up, how many outs are there, what's the score, who's up," Johnson said. "There are just too many things going on that you have to think about and be ready to react to to think about the enormity or the pressure or the magnitude of the game. That happens before the game. During the game, you just go out and play."

That's what he did. Johnson was not a strikeout pitcher or one with perfect control. He simply tried to throw strikes and let nature take its course. He retired 11 straight batters after giving up the first-inning single and relied on letting the batters hit the ball up into the air. Johnson went seven innings plus one batter and allowed just two runs on two hits. Seventeen of the 21 outs he recorded that day were on pop ups or fly balls.

"I was very fortunate," Johnson said. "I realized the dome was open. They hit a [few] fly balls in the first two or three innings that didn't go out that I thought were home runs. I realized, 'Just throw it over, I don't think anybody can hit home runs today.' I just threw fastballs over the plate and let them hit it."

The Orioles had a 3-1 lead when he left after a very strong effort. But the bullpen fell apart in the eighth, letting the Blue Jays score three runs to win. However, Johnson gained a lot of confidence from that short stint with the Orioles and how well he did in those big games. He had career bests the following year with a 13-9 record in 29 starts and became one of Baltimore's best starters.

Johnson faded after that, only staying in the majors two more years. But he learned enough from the game to work on teaching his son, staying with the Orioles in different capacities, and still finding fun in the game. He still loves baseball and is glad to be a part of the Orioles now.

He now works on various TV and radio shows about the Orioles, often with Tom Davis.

Where Have You Gone?

DICK HALL

Solid Relief

It's fair to say that life's been taxing for former Orioles relief pitcher Dick Hall since he retired after the 1971 season. But it's also fair to say that he doesn't mind.

Hall worked at becoming an accountant and got his CPA certificate two years before his playing career ended, and he stepped right into the new job, specializing in tax accounting and staying there until he retired from the full-time work life at the age of 71 in 2001. He recently was working just the tax season and still living in the Baltimore area.

Playing in Baltimore brought Hall the most success in his career. He pitched for Pittsburgh and the Kansas City A's before coming to the Orioles in 1961. Hall stayed with the Orioles, playing on the surprise 1966 World Series champions before being traded to the Phillies after the season. The Baltimore pitching staff was so dominant in that World Series against the Dodgers that Hall never even got into a game.

The Phillies released him after the 1968 season, and Baltimore re-signed him for the following year. Hall stayed with the Orioles for the final three years of his career as Baltimore became the American League's dominant team.

The six-foot-six Hall had an unusual pitching motion, where he moved all over the place, almost seeming to squat as he threw. A Washington sportswriter once described it as looking like "a drunken giraffe on roller skates." Hall still scratches his head in trying to figure out how he wound up pitching that way.

#29 DICK HALL • P
Seasons with the Orioles: 1961-1966, 1969-1971

Best Season with the Orioles: 1970
Highlight Stats from that Season: He played a large role in helping the Orioles win the 1970 American League championship and then the World Series. Hall went 10-5 in just 32 relief appearances and had a 3.08 ERA. Hall also got the win in Game 1 of the ALCS with 4⅔ innings of long re-lief against Minnesota and added a save in the second game of the World Series in Cincinnati.

"I've decided that most of it was genetics, that was the way I could throw easiest," Hall said. "I've got a grandson who pitches Little League now, and his motion is closer to mine than anything I've ever seen."

Hall said he thinks the unusual motion did help a little more than he realized.

"I talked a little bit to some of the other ballplayers who faced me, and they said they had trouble picking the ball up," Hall said. "As I threw, I fell a little bit to the right."

Manager Earl Weaver used Hall during his final three years in what would be called a setup role now. Relief pitching was different in those days, not like today, where getting lefty-lefty and righty-righty matchups seems to be the rule rather than the exception. During Hall's final three years, the Orioles used Pete Richert and Eddie Watt as their short men with the tall righty coming in before that.

"Back then, if I came in in the seventh inning, and if I didn't get into trouble, I finished the game," Hall said. "That was basically my role."

With a strong starting staff that included, at times, people like Jim Palmer, Dave McNally, Mike Cuellar, Pat Dobson, and others, Hall and the Baltimore relievers weren't often called upon. But Hall did a good job in key situations, specifically in the 1970 playoffs.

Hall came in during Game 1 of the American League Championship Series with Minnesota when starting pitcher Cuellar found himself in trouble. The left-hander already had hit a wind-aided grand slam, but he couldn't get out of the fifth inning. Hall came on with one out and pitched the final 4⅔ innings to help Baltimore pull out a 10-6 win. The Orioles then went on to sweep the series and earn a World Series date with the Cincinnati Reds.

Hall helped rescue Cuellar again in Game 2 of the World Series in Cincinnati. The Big Red Machine battered Cuellar early, taking a 4-0 lead in the second inning. The Orioles battled back and took a 6-4 lead. Hall came on and pitched the final 2⅓ innings and got the save as Baltimore pulled out a 6-5 victory for a 2-0 lead in the Series. That win proved crucial as it let the Orioles go back for three games at home and in charge of a Series, which they won in five games.

Hall said that was one of his bigger career thrills. He also enjoyed pitching for the Orioles against Roger Maris in the final days of the famous 1961 season when the Yankees right fielder made his run at Babe Ruth's record of 60 homers in a season. Maris wanted to break the record in 154 games, like Ruth did, to avoid having the infamous asterisk next to his name in the baseball record books.

New York played at Baltimore in a series where the Yankees actually got to game number 154. Right-hander Milt Pappas started for the Orioles and gave up an early homer to Maris—number 59 on the season. Pappas couldn't get it going that night, and Hall came in early. He wound up throwing 5⅔ innings of shutout relief and struck out Maris once and got him to fly to right the other time. The New York right fielder came close on the second at-bat, ripping a pitch deep to right field, but it wound up just another out as he ended the 154th game with 59 homers.

"Every pitch was a low outside fastball," Hall said. "I knew he'd try to pull them. He was really diving into it, but [the ball to right field] wasn't high enough. I could tell right away."

Hall also remembers the 1969 World Series where the Amazing Mets shocked the baseball world by beating the Orioles in five games to win the title.

"They had good pitching, and our team batting average was around .160, and that's what cost us," Hall said. "[Ron] Swoboda made that great catch [in Game 4], and had we batted .240 and scored some more runs, things might [have been different]. If you hit .160, you're lucky to get any runs."

Hall said he had little trouble adjusting to life after baseball. He moved right into being a CPA and worked in the Baltimore area until he retired from full-time work. Hall was fortunate—he found two careers that he enjoyed and did well in both.

"They're pretty different," Hall said of baseball and being a CPA. "I'd say [baseball] is a real goldfish bowl existence. With tax returns, they can catch mistakes and fix them. But in baseball, if you make a bad pitch and a guy hits a home run, there's not the slightest thing you can do to fix it."

Not much apparently changed for Hall after the publication of the initial version of this book. *The Baltimore Sun* reported a few years ago that he was still doing some part-time work as an accountant and playing golf.

Where Have You Gone?

KEN SINGLETON

Singy

K en Singleton still loves to talk about baseball.
He was one of the best outfielders/hitters the Baltimore Orioles had
during the 1970s and 1980s after coming to town in a big trade after the
1974 season that sent longtime Baltimore pitcher Dave McNally to Montreal. Singleton is a rare personality, which lets him talk with people and
make them feel at ease—and fans loved him.

He stayed with the Orioles for the rest of his career and then moved to
the television booth, first working on Montreal games before becoming a
Yankees commentator. Singleton has been in the booth for about 20 years,
but still makes his home in Baltimore, and fans voted him as one of the
franchise's 50 all-time favorite Orioles at the end of the 2004 season.

Singleton still must follow baseball because of his job—and also to keep
an eye on his son, Justin. Justin played for the Class AA Eastern League
champion New Hampshire Fisher Cats in 2004 and split time between that
team and Class AAA Syracuse during 2005. He played in the minors and
independent league through 2007.

He is one of the players that Ken Singleton loves to talk about.

"He's a good player, and he can do some things that I couldn't do,"
said the proud father. "He can really play. I got to see him play a couple of
games [in 2004], and I was fortunate enough that the two I went to, he hit
a home run in each game."

Justin Singleton is a strong defensive player who's a center fielder. Ken
Singleton didn't have the speed needed for that position and spent most of
his time in right field and doing whatever was needed to help the Orioles.

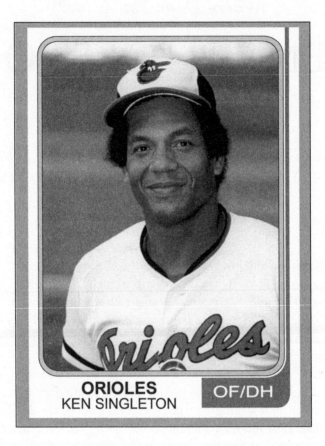

ORIOLES
KEN SINGLETON
OF/DH

Best Season with the Orioles: 1979
Highlight Stats from that Season: Singleton hit 35 homers and had 111 RBI that season. He also hit .295 and made the All-Star Game. Also, for good measure, Singleton batted .375 in the American League Championship Series and followed that with a .357 effort in the World Series versus Pittsburgh.

He could hit and had a great eye and a knack for coming up with key hits in key situations.

"It was enjoyable to come to the ballpark, because I was on a good team every year," Singleton said. "Every game meant something. I found out recently that during the 10 years I was here, the O's had the best record in baseball during the regular season. It's quite an accomplishment when you think about it."

Singleton said that one of the keys for the Orioles to stay strong on a regular basis was that the crux of the team remained the same for a long time.

"I got to play with some quality people," Singleton said. "In those days, the turnover wasn't quite like it is now, so that the teams had a chance to stick together. I think the players on our team realized we had a good situation, and nobody really wanted to leave."

Singleton had some big years with an Orioles team that won many games. He started his career with the New York Mets. A first-round pick in the 1967 amateur draft, Singleton played with the Mets during 1970 and 1971 before going to the Montreal Expos just before the start of the 1972 season in the deal that brought Rusty Staub to the Mets.

He played with Montreal for three years and slumped badly in 1974, which possibly led the Expos to look at making a move. Singleton had an unusual problem during that season, missing a few weeks in midseason after discovering that he suffered an allergy to materials in the Montreal uniform. But he came to Baltimore that winter, a move that paid off handsomely for both Singleton and the Orioles.

Singleton played 10 seasons with Baltimore and became a powerful part of the Orioles lineup. Many expected Singleton to be a No. 3- or No. 5-type hitter when coming to town, but manager Earl Weaver surprised everyone at first by putting him in the leadoff spot on a regular basis. The Orioles were loaded with a number of talented outfielders that season, including Al Bumbry, Paul Blair, Don Baylor, and Jim Northrup, so Weaver had to move everyone around to get them at-bats.

But Weaver often kept Singleton in the top spot, a puzzling move to some because the outfielder didn't exactly fit the bill of the conventional leadoff hitter. He didn't have the speed that managers love to have, but the Orioles loved Singleton's eye. He knew how to draw walks and could hit with power and set the table. By season's end, Singleton drew 118 walks, scored 86 runs, and still hit 15 homers with 55 RBI along with a .300 average.

Singleton's power then slowly began to emerge over the next few seasons. His best year came in 1979 when he finished with 35 homers and 111 RBI plus 109 walks and 93 runs. Singleton finished with a .295 average, and the Orioles won the American League pennant before falling to the Pittsburgh Pirates in the World Series. He batted .375 in the American League Championship Series against California and then hit .357 versus Pittsburgh—and later finished second in the American League Most Valuable Player voting.

He stayed with the Orioles through the 1984 season, setting a club record with 10 straight hits at one point and eventually retiring at the age of 37. Singleton went straight to the broadcast booth after his career ended. He spent several years with the Expos, working until the late 1990s when he moved to the Yankees booth. Singleton works about 95 games per year for New York, but still lives in Baltimore, the town where he had his greatest success in baseball.

"It wasn't hard, it was just something I had to get used to doing, and I really enjoy my job," Singleton said. "It's been a lot of fun. I've worked with Joe Torre and his coaching staff and some quality players. It's been fun in that respect. Then the season's over, and I can do what I want."

Singleton said he needs about three hours to prepare for a game. He'll arrive at around 3:30 p.m. for a 7 p.m. contest to go over the notes and get everything ready. He treats it just as seriously as he did things during his playing days.

"You have to like what you're doing. If you do your homework and you're prepared, you should be fine," Singleton said. "You can draw on your own experience, and that's what the fans want to hear about."

Singleton loves talking about baseball, but realized that simply running one's mouth isn't enough to be a good analyst. He works hard, studying info about the Yankees and their opponents. He spends time between assignments following the Yankees and baseball.

"I think that what happens to a lot of players... is they think that just being themselves is good enough," Singleton said. "But it's not. That's where the preparation comes in."

Singleton remains a regular broadcaster with the Yankees TV network.

GREGG OLSON

Throwing a Curve

When Gregg Olson came up to the Orioles in 1989, he immediately became a star. He had a cup of coffee with the team at the end of a horrible 1988 season when Baltimore was the worst team in baseball, but the Orioles took a chance and made him their closer for 1989.

It was a move they never regretted. Olson won Rookie of the Year honors that season and became one of baseball's best closers for the next several seasons. Olson stayed with the Orioles through the 1993 season when arm problems slowed him and sent the right-hander on a journey that led to seven more teams—even becoming a closer once more later in his career—but he never quite became the pitcher he was in his early days in Baltimore.

Olson's major league career ended when the Dodgers released him in 2001.

Olson had been relaxing for a while since leaving the playing field, but had been hoping to find his way back to the diamond.

The best parts of his career happened in Baltimore, especially in the early days. The six-foot-four, 206-pound right-hander became a dominant closer almost immediately. Olson had a good fastball and a curveball that often buckled batters' knees and froze their bats. He also had good control with all of his pitches and finished 5-2 with a sparkling 1.69 ERA the first season, a time he enjoyed very much.

"Baltimore was my first big league stint, and I played in Memorial Stadium," Olson said. "It was like you knew all the fans and everyone knew you. It was a wonderful place to play."

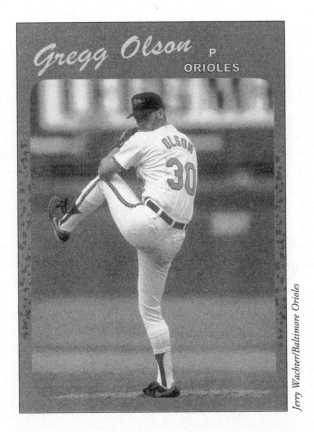

Gregg Olson P
ORIOLES

Jerry Wachter/Baltimore Orioles

#30 GREGG OLSON • P
Seasons with the Orioles: 1989-1993

Best Season with the Orioles: 1989
Highlight Stats from that Season: Olson won American League Rookie of
the Year honors with a 5-2 record and 27 saves in his debut as the Orioles'
closer. He combined a knee-buckling curveball with great control and a
good fastball to strike out 90 batters in 85 innings
and finish with a 1.69 ERA.

However, one of Olson's most remembered moments that year was a sad one and came in the final weekend. The Orioles had been baseball's surprise team that year, bouncing back after losing 107 games the year before to lead the American League East for much of that season. They came into the final weekend of the season fighting Toronto for the division title.

The Blue Jays had taken over and held a one-game lead with three games left. The first game of the crucial series was on Friday night in Toronto, and the Orioles took a 1-0 lead when Phil Bradley homered to lead off the game in the first. But the Blue Jays couldn't do much with Orioles starter Jeff Ballard, who clung to the one-run lead through seven innings.

Olson replaced Ballard with one out and one on in the eighth. Pinch runner Tom Lawless stole second and moved to third on a ground out. Olson was one out away from escaping the inning, but then uncorked a wild pitch that got past catcher Jamie Quirk, letting the tying run in. Toronto went on to score a 2-1 win in 11 innings. The Blue Jays then clinched the division title with a win the next day.

Olson said the pressure never really bothered him, because he wasn't experienced enough to realize all that was happening around him.

"I didn't know any better," Olson said. "I didn't know [that] I was too young, and I wasn't supposed to be doing that. I just knew that my whole life I'd had success and just assumed that I'd keep going. There was so much pressure in that role. I didn't know I [wasn't] supposed to be doing it. I just went out, and I was just me."

He bounced back with solid seasons the next few years, getting 37 saves in 1990 and making the All-Star team. Olson added 31, 36, and 29 saves in 1991, 1992, and 1993, respectively. However, Olson began having some problems. He had a 3.18 ERA in 1991 and went 1-5 in 1992. The biggest problem came late in the 1993 season—and it involved his elbow.

Olson said he always wound up taking about a week off midway through each season—around late July or early August—to deal with the tendinitis. But in 1993, Olson said he took it too far. He tried to push through the soreness and blew it out one night.

"I thought I got back to 90 or 95 percent, but in doing that I screwed up my mechanics and it cost me the next year, because I was just horrible," Olson said.

He went on the disabled list in late August 1993 because of the soreness, which was later reportedly diagnosed as a torn ligament. An Associated Press story later in Olson's career said that doctors advised him to have it surgically repaired, but Olson knew that could cost him the 1994 season, something he didn't really want to deal with. The story said that Olson spoke to Nolan Ryan, who advised him that he had recovered from a similar injury by using a tough rehab program. Olson adopted it and worked hard on getting better throughout that winter.

He became a free agent after the 1993 season, and Atlanta signed him for 1994. Olson struggled throughout that season, pitching in just 16 games with an astronomical 9.20 ERA.

"In doing everything to make myself strong and protect the area that was injured, I overlooked my mechanics," he said in an Associated Press story. "I got into spring training with the Braves and I was way behind. I tried to push it a little bit, and I ended up pulling a muscle right in front of the elbow. I was on the DL for two months with that."

Mike Devereaux and Gregg Olson

Olson then began to bounce to different teams after that. He then pitched for Cleveland, Kansas City, Detroit, Houston, Minnesota, Kansas City (again), Arizona, and Los Angeles. But he kept working and had a good comeback during his two-year stint with the Diamondbacks in 1998 and 1999.

Olson went 3-4 with 30 saves in 1998. He followed that with a 9-4 record the following year, posting 14 saves and helping Arizona make the National League playoffs. The Diamondbacks lost to the Mets in the first round, but Olson enjoyed being a closer once again.

"I don't know if everything came back or I got smarter or what it was," Olson said. "But something worked, and nothing was ever the same as it was before I got hurt [however]."

Olson said that looking back at his career, Baltimore and Arizona were the teams that brought him the most joy.

"Baltimore and Arizona were my two favorite places," Olson said. "Baltimore was my first big league stint, and I played in Memorial Stadium. It was like you knew all the fans and everyone knew you. It was a wonderful place to play."

Olson owns Toolshed Sports and wrote the book *We Got to Play Baseball*. In addition, Olson has been a scout with the San Diego Padres and worked with the Orioles during Spring Training in 2013.

Where Have You Gone?

EDDIE MURRAY

Despite the Silence, the Bat Spoke Volumes

E ddie Murray truly was an enigma during his times in Baltimore. He won the American League Rookie of the Year award in 1977, became one of baseball's best players, and eventually was elected into the Baseball Hall of Fame during his first year of eligibility in 2003. He was someone whose abilities were respected by all throughout his career.

But not many people knew Murray outside of the clubhouse. A shy, quiet type who often directed reporters to talk to other players, Murray eventually stopped talking to all reporters following a critical article written about him in the mid-1980s. Murray took offense to some comments from then-owner Edward Bennett Williams and basically stopped talking to all Baltimore media.

When the Orioles traded Murray to Los Angeles following the 1988 season, he didn't want to talk to Baltimore-area writers at the press conference announcing the deal, upsetting a few more people. When Murray came back to Baltimore later in his career during the 1996 season, helping the Orioles to their first postseason appearance in 13 years, he hit his 500th home run at Oriole Park. But he still almost never talked to the media on the record. He'd banter with reporters a little here and there, but wouldn't change.

Many think that's what has hurt him in his post-playing career—his attempt to become a major league manager. Murray was a solid coach for the Orioles and Cleveland Indians after retiring in 1998, but when he interviewed for the Baltimore managing job in the fall of 2003, some wondered how he'd do handling the daily grind of dealing with the media. Managers typically talk with the media a few hours before and then right after every

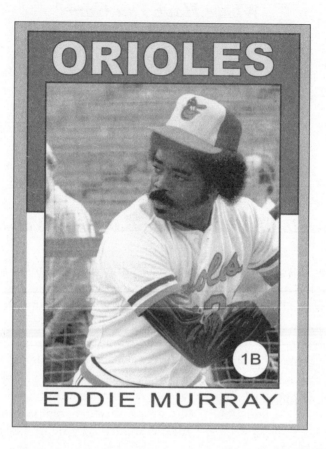

ORIOLES

1B

EDDIE MURRAY

Best Season with the Orioles: 1983
Highlight Stats from that Season: The Hall of Famer did a little bit of everything that season. He hit 33 homers and had 111 RBI and finished with a .306 average. The first baseman also won Gold Glove and Silver Slugger honors, made the All-Star Game, and added three homers in post-season play as the Orioles won the World Series.

game, and there were thoughts about how Murray would be able to handle that on a daily basis, especially because at some point he'd get upset about something like nearly every manager or coach.

But Murray pulled a surprise and met with the media after interviewing for the managing job. In fact, he was funny and handled the give-and-take beautifully and was considered to be a leading candidate for the job for a long time before Lee Mazzilli swooped in out of nowhere and surprised Orioles officials with a great interview and won the position.

Murray then went back to serving as the Cleveland batting coach under Eric Wedge as the Indians tried to rebuild after having to overhaul their team. But Murray was fired midway through the 2005 season.

Murray's baseball career appeared up in the air after he lost the Cleveland job in 2005, but it got another boost when new manager Grady Little hired him as the hitting coach for the Los Angeles Dodgers for 2006 season.

Murray had been the hitting coach with the Orioles and was very much respected for his knowledge. Although he still rarely spoke to the media, it was easy to see how much the players thought of him, because they'd stop immediately and pay attention whenever he'd walk into the clubhouse. Murray would stand in the back part of the clubhouse near the lockers of players like David Segui, and all eyes would turn his way.

That kind of attention was fine with Murray. But media attention was a different story. Murray never wanted much media attention from the start of his career in 1977. He was a third-round pick in the 1973 draft and came to the big leagues when the Orioles already had a solid first baseman named Lee May. But the Orioles couldn't ignore his talents. Murray could hit for average and power from both sides of the plate, and team officials knew they had to get his bat into the lineup in some form.

So while May worked with him a lot behind the scenes, tutoring a player he knew would be taking his job eventually, Murray spent much of his time at designated hitter during his rookie year, playing 111 games in that spot and getting into 160 games overall. He won Rookie of the Year honors in 1977, finishing with a .283 average plus 27 homers and 88 RBI.

That began a long career marked by consistency. Murray was an eight-time All-Star who finished with a .287 career average and 504 home runs during 21 seasons in the big leagues. He won the Gold Glove at first base three different times, although many felt he should have won more. He also finished in the top five of the league's Most Valuable Player voting five times, taking second twice.

He often hit well in postseason play, but he struggled at times during three World Series appearances. Murray batted .258 in nine postseason

Cal Ripken Jr. and Eddie Murray

series overall but hit just .169 in three World Series appearances. He batted .154 in the 1979 World Series where the Orioles blew a 3-1 lead in games and watched Pittsburgh pull out a seven-game triumph.

In that Series, Murray hit several balls hard—that went right at people, including a shot in Game 7 that appeared headed for extra bases but hung up in the air and let right fielder Dave Parker get to it.

Murray then had problems throughout the 1983 World Series, but his bat awakened at the right time. He blasted two homers in Game 5 at Philadelphia, sparking the Orioles to a 5-0 victory and letting them clinch the Series. Murray batted .250 in that Series. He had more problems playing for the Indians in the 1995 Series, batting just .105 while going two for 19. However, several Cleveland hitters stumbled in that Series, and Atlanta won it.

Murray's career ended a year later, and he was an easy first-ballot Hall of Fame pick in 2003. By that time, Murray had already been building a reputation as a respected hitting coach and surprised a few people with a touching speech at the Hall of Fame induction ceremonies.

He went for the Orioles job a few months later and spoke to the media some more. There were signs that his self-imposed wall was coming down. The more Murray wants to become a manager, the more that will help him. But it's interesting to wonder how much that would have helped him earlier on.

The best example of Murray came when he returned to Aberdeen, Maryland, the hometown of longtime friend Cal Ripken Jr., to help honor his buddy on the 10th anniversary of Ripken tying Lou Gehrig's consecutive games record. With several media people sitting in the dugout at Ripken Stadium, Murray was asked about coming back.

He looked at the writers, smiled, and said, "Time flies."

One of the few times that Murray actually came out and spoke in public was at the funeral of former bullpen coach/catcher Elrod Hendricks in late December 2005.

Hendricks and Lee May served as a mentor to the quiet Murray when he came up to the major leagues in 1977. Murray said with a chuckle, when eulogizing Hendricks, that Hendricks and May played "good cop/bad cop" with him, drawing laughter from several of his former Orioles teammates seated in front.

Murray told several stories of how Hendricks knew how to make him laugh, make him relax, and just enjoy the game.

"What a man," Murray said. "He has taught me so much [that] got me through a lot of things. It was special. Ellie was a super person."

He served as a coach with the Dodgers until 2007, but never got a chance to manage in the majors. The Orioles honored him in 2012 by unveiling a statue at the ballpark. He also ran into some off-the-field problems and had to settle an SEC suit involving insider trading. Murray never was charged or indicted in the case and denied doing anything wrong.

STORM DAVIS

Still Just a Regular Guy

W hen Storm Davis came to the Orioles as a 20-year-old rookie in the 1982 season, he attracted a lot of notice for several reasons. First came the unmistakable resemblance to star Jim Palmer in many ways. Both were long and lean and could throw great fastballs. Many called Davis the second coming of Palmer and kept waiting for him to pitch just like the Hall of Famer.

There also were the looks. Davis made the hearts of many female fans flutter just like Palmer did. Tall, tanned, and with a great smile plus an easy-going personality, Davis came off strikingly similar to Palmer.

Then there was the name. Not many people named "Storm" had come through Baltimore. Truth is his real name was George Earl Davis Jr., with "Storm" coming from a book his mother read and loved—called *Doctors on Trial*—while pregnant with him.

But Davis was different. There wasn't much Storm associated with this man. He was a more low-key, very religious man who not only didn't seek the spotlight, he kind of stayed away from it. He let his pitching do the talking, and although he was not another Jim Palmer, Davis became a very strong pitcher who threw in the majors for 13 years and won 113 games.

When his career ended, Davis didn't head for the broadcast booth like many players do now. He went back home to Jacksonville and spent much of his time coaching high school baseball and football while watching his three children grow up.

"I just love working with kids; it's a passion for me," Davis said. "It's easy for me to do, and it's natural for me to work with the kids because I just love coaching. I really do."

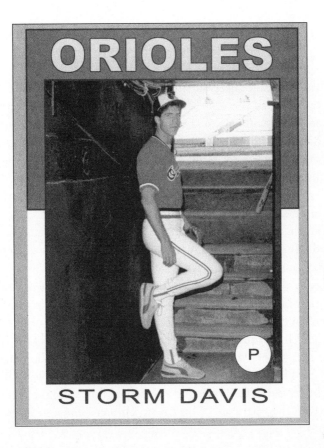

ORIOLES

STORM DAVIS

P

#34 STORM DAVIS • P
Seasons with the Orioles: 1982-1986, 1992

Best Season with the Orioles: 1984
Highlight Stats from that Season: Davis had a solid 14-9 record with a
3.12 ERA for a struggling Orioles team in 1984. He threw a career-best
225 innings and allowed only seven home runs and had a career-best 10
complete games in 31 starts.

Davis takes a lot of pride in his work with the kids, including a stint at the Trinity Christian Academy, where he was the head baseball coach and also the football team's offensive line coach.

The baseball team made the final eight in Class 2-A in Florida while the football team lost in the state semifinals—after winning the state championship the two previous years. Davis does things that a former pro baseball player who pitched in two World Series wouldn't be expected to do. As an assistant coach, he breaks down game film for the football team and then later works with the linemen on various tactics.

Davis said he understands what this entails as he's the son of a coach, and to him, it's something that's just a whole lot of fun.

"I like to teach what's been taught to me, to teach what I've learned," Davis said. "It's a great calling in life to be a teacher. I go over to the school in the afternoons... and help coach the teams."

Davis was also at the Bolles School for six years before working at Trinity Christian as head baseball coach. Davis appreciates the importance of teaching from his father's experiences, but also from some of how the more experienced Orioles players helped him during the early days of his career.

Davis remembers vividly how Jim Palmer gave him the benefit of his vast wealth of knowledge throughout those tough first days. Palmer could have made life tough for Davis and not helped him since the future Hall of Famer was in the final part of his career. Palmer helped some more as the Orioles headed back to Baltimore for the final weekend of the 1982 season. He spent lots of time with Davis as the team returned home, telling him exactly how to pitch to every hitter in the dangerous Milwaukee lineup.

The Orioles closed that season with an emotional four-game series against the division-leading Brewers as Baltimore was three games back with four games to play and needed to sweep a Friday night doubleheader to stay alive. The Orioles did just that with Davis going the distance to win the second game, relying heavily on the knowledge Palmer fed him to do well. Davis later pitched in the World Series for the Oakland A's but still says that Milwaukee moment with the Orioles was one of the highlights of his career.

"That was by far my most exciting moment," Davis said. "I threw a complete game, and that was the most important game. I was too young and too naïve that I just don't think it got to me."

Davis still shakes his head at the way Palmer seemed to know every detail. Even now, decades after retiring from the game, Palmer speaks on Orioles television broadcasts of the right way to pitch this guy from his playing days or what pitch he threw in that situation.

"He sat with me the whole flight back [before the Milwaukee series] and talked about how to get them out, and he was right, he was exactly right," Davis said. "He was able to know when to go out of the zone, when to elevate the ball, when to pitch inside, and he sat with me on the whole flight back and talked about how to get them out."

Many wondered if the pressure of being compared so closely to Palmer affected Davis during his days with the Orioles, but he says it didn't.

"I wasn't as talented as Jim, and that was obvious," Davis said. "But I think we were both similar pitchers in that we were both fastball pitchers."

Davis has ventured into the world of minor league baseball, serving as a pitching coach the last few years. He was with the Hickory Crawdads (Class A) in the Texas organization before moving to the Daytona Cubs (Chicago organization) in 2013, when that team won the Florida State League title.

Where Have You Gone?

MIKE CUELLAR

A Great Trade

Mike Cuellar became one of the most respected and feared pitchers in the American League during his stint with the Orioles. He loved pitching, was great in big games, and had a screwball most hitters couldn't touch.

For many years, Cuellar waited and hoped to eventually find the success he did on the mound as a coach. Several pitchers who did well with the Orioles wound up working with pitchers after being out of the game for a while.

Cuellar came to the Orioles after the 1968 season. Many Orioles fans scratched their heads when the team traded for the Houston pitcher. The Orioles had to give up a popular player—Curt Blefary—in the deal, and although Cuellar certainly was a good pitcher, he never seemed to be able to find his way. The Astros were the fifth major league organization he'd pitched for, and some wondered what the Orioles were getting.

But Cuellar changed upon coming to Baltimore, becoming one of baseball's best pitchers during his eight-year stint. The left-hander with the screwball that often tied opposing batters in knots won numerous big games, tied for a Cy Young Award, and earned three All-Star Game berths. The trade truly turned out to be a steal.

Cuellar made his first All-Star Game appearance in 1967 during a 16-11 season with the Astros. But he slid backward the following year, going just 8-11 in 24 starts. The Orioles, meanwhile, were looking for pitching and hoping to challenge the world champion Detroit Tigers in 1969.

Their starting rotation had been questionable at the end of 1968. The addition of Cuellar and the return of young phenom Jim Palmer after two

142

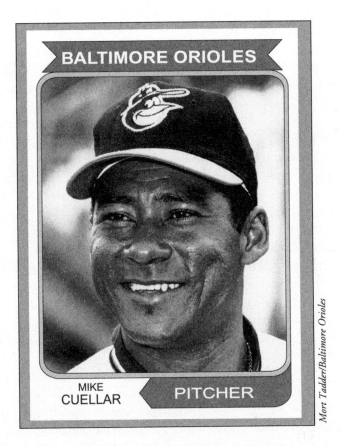

BALTIMORE ORIOLES

MIKE
CUELLAR   PITCHER

Mort Tadder/Baltimore Orioles

#35 MIKE CUELLAR • P
Seasons with the Orioles: 1969-1976

Best Season with the Orioles: 1969
Highlight Stats from that Season: Cuellar made a fast impact when coming to Baltimore after an offseason deal with Houston. The left-hander posted a 23-11 record with an impressive 2.38 ERA in 290⅔ innings. He also won Game 1 of the World Series against the Mets and became one of baseball's top left-handers as few batters could figure out his screwball.

seasons of arm troubles jolted the rotation upward. Right-hander Jim Hardin was a starter and won 18 games in 1968, but got pushed to the bottom of the rotation, making only 20 starts in 1969 while Palmer made 23 and went 16-4. Palmer missed several weeks with arm injuries, but that was the turning point in his career.

The addition of Cuellar truly gave the Orioles one of the strongest rotations in baseball. The left-hander fit right in with the Orioles and went 23-11 in 39 starts. He tossed 18 complete games and a monstrous total of 290⅔ innings, performances that helped him earn a tie for the prestigious Cy Young Award with Detroit's Denny McLain—who'd won 31 games the previous year.

"We had a great team," Cuellar said. "We rooted for each other. That's the key right there. It was just a good group."

When Frank Robinson joined the team in 1966 following a big trade with Cincinnati, he eventually set up a "Kangaroo Court," a comedic thing that happened after each Orioles victory. Robinson wore a silly wig, and team members were fined for doing little things like throwing to the wrong base. Cuellar said the closeness the team found from activities like that helped the Orioles grow.

"Everybody [pulled] for everybody else," Cuellar said. "It was just great. That's one big thing. When you've got a team like that, it's tough to lose."

Cuellar then began a strong run of postseason appearances. He started in Game 1 of the first American League Championship Series against Minnesota in Baltimore. The left-hander gave up just three runs on three hits in eight innings, but the Orioles had to rally to tie the game in the ninth and pulled out a 4-3 win in the 12th on Paul Blair's perfect squeeze bunt.

Cuellar fared even better when starting Game 1 of the World Series, going the distance in a 4-1 victory over the New York Mets. He turned in another strong effort in Game 4, allowing only one run in seven innings before leaving with a no-decision as New York pulled out a controversial 2-1 victory that set up its Series-clinching win the following day.

Overall, Cuellar had a spectacular World Series, allowing only two runs in 16 innings. He came back with an even better year in 1970, going 24-8 in 297⅔ innings. This was before the specialized relievers era of today, and Cuellar became a pitcher who the Orioles could depend upon to get them late into games. He also finished with 21 complete games.

He didn't do quite as well in the postseason, but still had some big moments. Cuellar hit a wind-blown grand slam in Game 1 of the 1970 ALCS at Minnesota that helped the Orioles score seven runs in the fourth and take a 9-2 lead. However, the Twins rocked Cuellar for six runs and 10 hits

2004

in 4⅓ innings—and he couldn't finish the fifth and get the win as Baltimore got a strong relief effort from Dick Hall in a 10-6 victory.

Cuellar struggled again in his first start during the 1970 World Series with Cincinnati. With the Orioles holding a 1-0 lead in the Series, Cuellar couldn't get out of the third inning, giving up four runs on four hits in 2⅓ innings. But the Orioles rallied for a 6-5 win that proved crucial. Cuellar then got another chance in Game 5 with the Orioles needing just one win to wrap it up.

Once again, Cuellar started poorly. He gave up three runs in the top of the first inning, and manager Earl Weaver said later that he was one batter away from pulling Cuellar with two outs and three runs in. Cuellar then retired Tommy Helms and then set down 16 of the next 17 batters as the Orioles rallied again for a 9-3 victory that gave them their second World Series title in five years.

Cuellar continued to be one of the Orioles' strong pitchers over the next five years, as Baltimore remained one of baseball's best teams. He won 92 games over the next five years with Baltimore, including some stellar postseason performances. The Orioles released Cuellar after he slid to a 4-13 record in 1976. He pitched two games for the California Angels in 1977 before retiring.

Cuellar died in 2010 after battling cancer. He'd been doing some volunteer coaching with the Orioles in Spring Training since he settled in Florida.

Where Have You Gone?

TOM PHOEBUS

Local Boy Makes Good

E very now and then, one of Tom Phoebus's elementary students would come up to him and say something to the effect of "Hey, you pitched in the major leagues." Phoebus would pretty much just laugh and say something to the effect of "Yeah, you're right."

Phoebus didn't try to constantly tell students, "Hey, I was a major league pitcher." He is a low-key personality who grew up in Baltimore and did what every kid would love to do—he went on to pitch for his favorite team. The right-hander pitched for the Orioles and even threw a no-hitter before moving on to a teaching career and, later in 2003, retiring to a life of relaxation.

While growing up, Phoebus went to Mount St. Joseph High School—a private school that's long been a baseball power in Baltimore—in high school and playing for the Gaels and Leone's amateur team, one of the nation's top baseball squads. He eventually made it to the Orioles, pitching for them.

Phoebus went 14-9 in 1967 and won the Rookie of the Year award after tying a major league record by throwing two shutouts in his first two starts at the end of the 1966 season. The Orioles went to the World Series that year and swept the Dodgers, but Phoebus wasn't on the postseason roster.

He had another strong year in 1968 with a 15-15 record with a career-best 2.62 ERA and another career best with 240⅔ innings. Phoebus then stayed in the starting rotation when the Orioles won the American League in 1969, posting a 14-7 record, but did not get into the World Series versus the Mets where New York pulled its shocking upset.

He had 21 starts in 1970 when the Orioles won the World Series. Phoebus went only 5-5 that year, but pitched well in a crucial relief appearance

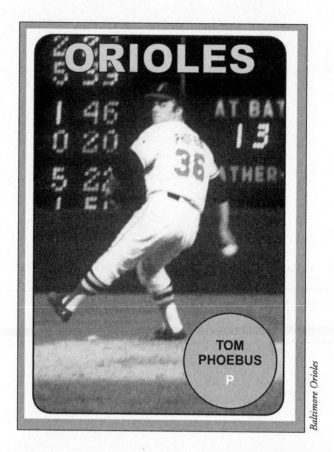

Baltimore Orioles

#36 TOM PHOEBUS • P
Seasons with the Orioles: 1966-1971

Best Season with the Orioles: 1967
Highlight Stats from that Season: The hometown boy quickly made his
mark as a rookie. Phoebus won *The Sporting News'* Rookie of the Year
award in 1967 with a 14-9 record and a 3.33 ERA in 33 starts
for the slumping Orioles.

in Game 2, getting the victory as the Orioles rallied for a 6-5 win in Cincinnati. The Orioles then traded him to San Diego in the deal that brought Pat Dobson to the team, and Phoebus pitched three more years in the majors.

He moved to Florida after baseball and made a new career as a physical education teacher. He went back to college at Manatee Community College and the University of South Florida, graduating in 1985 and teaching for 18 years in St. Lucie before retiring two years ago.

Phoebus said he would talk about his life in the majors if students asked him, and it was a subject that came up occasionally during his teaching career. He loved playing on some of the strong Orioles teams, but individually, the no-hitter was his shining moment.

"That was probably the biggest thing I did in [my career]," Phoebus said.

Phoebus already had started making a name for himself when he took the mound for the Orioles against the Boston Red Sox on April 27, 1968. The right-hander had won *The Sporting News'* American League Rookie of the Year honor the previous year, and the Orioles were expecting big things from him in 1968 as they tried to bounce back from a disappointing season.

The Red Sox, however, were coming off their spectacular "Impossible Dream" season where they shocked the baseball world by winning the American League in 1967. They were one of the best hitting teams in the game when Phoebus took the ball that Saturday afternoon, but everything went his way that day.

Phoebus pitched the only no-hitter of his major league career, helping the Orioles to a 6-0 victory over the Red Sox at Memorial Stadium. The right-hander struck out nine and walked three in a dominating performance—and had two hits and an RBI for good measure.

Phoebus also got an unusual break when Curt Blefary, an old friend from the minors, was penciled into the lineup at catcher due to injuries the Orioles had at the position. Blefary played only 40 games at catcher during his four years with the team, and this was one of the first. It was a move that Phoebus said proved to be a big one.

"I felt strong throughout the whole game, and Curt and I got along pretty well," Phoebus said. "He was a big, strong guy. I had a lot of confidence in him, and he had a lot of confidence in me."

Phoebus said that he had a good fastball, curveball, and slider, and could throw any of them whenever he needed.

"I felt like I could have pitched 12 or 13 innings," Phoebus said. "I had good stuff that day. Everything just went well."

The Orioles helped Phoebus by scoring four in the third inning for a quick 4-0 lead. They also added single runs in the fifth and eighth innings. Boston helped the Orioles with two timely errors that made four of the six runs unearned and proved costly to starter Gary Waslewski, who gave up five runs and eight hits in five innings.

Phoebus was in such command that Boston had only a few chances to break up the no-hitter. The best shot came in the eighth, but Brooks Robinson made a quick move to his left to stab a Rico Petrocelli liner. At that point, Phoebus knew where he stood with the no-hitter.

"From the seventh inning on, you try to do everything right," Phoebus said. "You just focus more the last couple of innings. From the seventh inning on, I knew I had a no-hitter, and I was just trying to get them out."

Phoebus closed the door in the ninth by striking out Boston third baseman Joe Foy. Carl Yastrzemski was waiting in the on-deck circle, but Phoebus finished off Foy and didn't have to worry about one of Boston's most famous hitters.

"I threw him a hard slider, but it broke up instead of away," Phoebus said. "The ball moved... but he was swinging for downtown and just missed."

And that was a subject that Phoebus, now retired, didn't mind talking about once more, a few decades after it happened.

According to a 2009 *Baltimore Sun* article, Phoebus was working on working out and staying in shape in Florida.

TERRY CROWLEY

Always Good in a Pinch

Terry Crowley was one of the Baltimore Orioles' best prospects when he made his way to the big club in the final month of the 1969 season. But Crowley dealt with something that many young players have to—he was on a club with too many good players and the team didn't want to let him go.

The left-handed hitter with the sweet swing could play first base and the outfield and later got some at-bats as a designated hitter. But the Orioles simply had too much talent, and Crowley couldn't break into the lineup on a consistent basis. However, the Staten Island native found a different way to make himself valuable—he became one of the game's better pinch hitters and situational players and stayed in the big leagues for parts of 15 seasons.

Crowley then took his hitting knowledge to another level after his playing career ended in 1983. He became one of the game's best batting coaches, having two stints with the Orioles along with a eight-year run with the Twins. He worked with the Orioles in the late 1980s before eventually landing in Minnesota from 1991 to 1998 and returned to Baltimore, where he's remained ever since, and many of the team's younger players credit him with making them better at their jobs.

A low-key personality, Crowley spent long stretches of time working with those who needed it. He's often seen heading into the batting cages that are between the clubhouse and Orioles dugout at Oriole Park at Camden Yards, doing the little things that helped young players like Luis Matos, Brian Roberts, or Walter Young grow.

"We have a nice group of young players," Crowley said of the 2005 Orioles. "They've done really well for us, and they've pretty much learned how

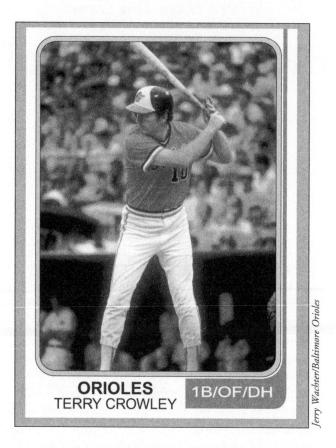

ORIOLES
TERRY CROWLEY
1B/OF/DH

Jerry Wachter/Baltimore Orioles

#37 TERRY CROWLEY • 1B/OF/DH
Seasons with the Orioles: 1969-1973, 1976-1982

Best Season with the Orioles: 1980
Highlight Stats from that Season: Crowley spent much of his career as a pinch hitter/situation player, but contributed the most in this season. He batted a career-best 288 with career highs in homers (12) and RBI (50), helping the Orioles battle the Yankees for first place much of that year.

to play every day, day in and day out, lefties, righties, play banged up, no days off."

Crowley understands more than most the need to always be prepared because he spent most of his time in the tough role of pinch hitter or situational player. He spent a lot of time on the bench waiting for managers like Earl Weaver to put him in and then tried to show them how valuable he could be—and more often than not he did just that.

However, it didn't mean Crowley loved it, especially after a solid minor league career where he was viewed as one of Baltimore's top hitting prospects.

"I hated it," Crowley said. "I used to make the All-Star team in the minors, year in and year out, and I got up here, and I wanted to play every day. But, as fate would have it, we had American League All-Stars at the positions that I played, so I had to wait my turn. And when it came time for my turn, I got traded. But that's a long time ago."

Crowley said now he realizes that it didn't work out so badly in the end.

"When I look back on it, I had almost 13 years as a player and had a couple of world championship rings," Crowley said.

He finally broke into the big leagues for a longer stretch with the 1970 Orioles at the age of 23. Crowley played in 83 games that year with just 152 at-bats—but hit .257 with five homers and 20 RBI. He didn't bat when the team swept the Twins in three games in that year's American League Championship Series and went oh for one in the Orioles' five-game win over the Reds in the World Series.

Crowley played only 18 games the next year before appearing to have a breakthrough season in 1972. The Orioles' three-year run of division and league titles ended with a team that was appearing to get older fast and suddenly couldn't score very many runs. Crowley played in a career-high 97 games and belted 11 homers and 10 doubles among his 57 hits. He hit .231 that season and slipped to .206 the next year before Texas purchased him after 1973.

But he never played for the Rangers in a regular-season game because the Reds bought his contract during spring training of 1974 and he was with them during Cincinnati's championship season of 1975. He went oh for one in the National League Championship Series and one for two in the thrilling seven-game World Series win over Boston.

The Reds then traded him to Atlanta in April 1976, and the Braves released him a month later. The Orioles then signed him 20 days after his release, and he stayed with the team in stretches from 1976 until the team released him in April 1983. He played his final year in the big leagues with Montreal.

Crowley's best year overall came with the 1980 Orioles as they battled

the Yankees for first place in the American League East throughout a long, hot summer. He batted .288 with career highs in homers (12), RBI (50), and hits (67) to help Baltimore.

Crowley also had two children who knew how to hit. Terry Jr. and Jimmy each were picked in the draft. The Orioles made Terry Jr. an eighth-round pick in the 1986 first-year player draft, and Jimmy was selected by the Red Sox in the 11th round in 1991. Jimmy was chosen after being picked as a coaches' All-American during his junior year at Clemson University. However, even though both were solid hitters, neither player made the major leagues.

But the older Crowley was fortunate to play on some gifted ball clubs, and despite not getting many regular chances to play, he contributed and saw some very good teams, especially some of the Orioles' and Reds' squads that ate up opponents and got wins in bunches.

"The best pitching team by far was the 1970 Orioles, and the best hitting team by far was the 1975 Reds," Crowley said. "The 1979 Orioles, even though I think we could have won the World Series but didn't, was probably the best mix of both, hitting, pitching, role players, defense, but offensively I don't think there will ever be a team put together like the 1975 Reds were."

But Crowley took all that he learned playing for those teams and used that to become the strong batting coach he now is with the Orioles.

Crowley also thinks that the fact that he wasn't an everyday five-star player might have helped him to become a better coach afterward. He talked about a theory that some people feel is true in all sports—a great player does not always make a great coach.

"I think that a good coach is not necessarily a guy who was a star when he played because stars have things laid out for them, they have very few setbacks in their career, and they play every day," Crowley said. "But when you take somebody who was just an average player, and you make him a coach, I think he knows a little bit about the ups and downs, the highs and the lows, he knows what it's like to take an oh for eight, what the mindset of the player is... and a lot of your superstars never did that. That's my opinion and that could be all hogwash, but I believe that to be true."

And then he smiled and went off to the batting cages to work with another young hitter.

Crowley grew into one of the most respected hitting coaches in Major League Baseball during his long career with the Orioles. He eventually stepped down from that position after 2010 to serve as a consultant with the team.

JOHN SHELBY

The T-Bone with the Cannon Arm

J ohn Shelby knew how to make a first impression with the Baltimore Orioles.

Shelby had slowly started seeing some time with the Orioles in the final days of the 1982 season as Baltimore was trying to make up a large deficit against the Milwaukee Brewers in the American League East. The Orioles knew Shelby was a solid defensive player, one who had a strong arm and could help them as they fought the Brewers.

But he made one play in the final week of the season that many in Baltimore still remember. Shelby made a perfect throw to home plate on a Cecil Cooper fly ball to nail Bob Skube and stop the Brewers from tying the game. Baltimore then scored twice in the ninth for a 5-2 win that left the Orioles with a good chance to try to tie them in the final week.

"I had a good arm, and I knew the only way [manager] Earl [Weaver] was going to put me in the game was if he felt like I had a chance to get somebody," Shelby said. "When we went back to Baltimore, the fans knew who I was. The fans had a sense of knowing who I was a little, and after the throw it seemed like everyone knew who I was."

Many in baseball have gotten to know him since then. Shelby—who had the nickname "T-Bone"—played in the majors through 1991 with the Orioles, Dodgers, and Tigers. He then went into coaching and managing, guiding teams in the Los Angeles minor league system for four years before moving up to the majors.

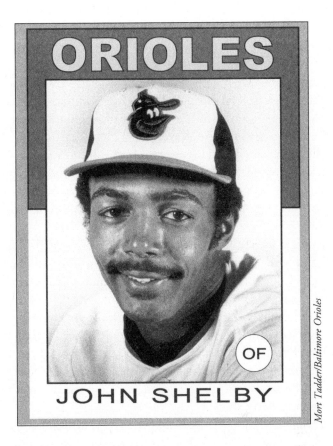

ORIOLES

OF

JOHN SHELBY

Mort Tadder/Baltimore Orioles

#37 JOHN SHELBY • OF
Seasons with the Orioles: 1981-1987

Best Season with the Orioles: 1983
Highlight Stats from that Season: This was Shelby's first full year in the major leagues, and he began to establish himself. He hit .258 with five homers and 27 RBI and 84 hits in 126 games, also often coming in for defense in games—and getting nine assists. In addition, Shelby hit .444 as the Orioles beat the Phillies in the World Series.

Shelby coached with the Dodgers for eight seasons, six as the first base coach, before moving to Pittsburgh for the 2006 season with manager Jim Tracy.

"John has a lot of experience at the major league level as a coach and as a player," Pittsburgh general manager Dave Littlefield told MLB.com. "He's a very upstanding man who relates well to players and understands what it takes to be a good major league player."

In addition, Shelby keeps his eye on his son, John, a former University of Kentucky player who's grown into one of the country's top players. He was named to the 2006 Wallace Watch List for the Brooks Wallace National Player of the Year Award that the College Baseball Foundation awards each season.

The younger Shelby led Kentucky in hits, homers, RBI, slugging percentages, and steals in one season. He was one of just two players in the Southeastern Conference to hit at least 10 homers (he finished with 10) and steal 20 bases (23).

The elder Shelby only showed that kind of big-time power in one season, hitting 21 in just 120 games after the Orioles traded him to the Dodgers in 1987. The Orioles selected him in the first round of the 1977 draft and were hoping for a Paul Blair-like player, the type they always loved in center field. Baltimore relied heavily on pitching and defense back then, and Shelby fit in perfectly.

Then, when Shelby made that big play in the Milwaukee game, it announced his arrival. If Milwaukee had scored on that play, momentum would have gone its way, and a Brewers win would have put the Orioles in serious trouble with one week to go. But Shelby knew right away that he might be able to pull off the play. He stayed still when the ball was hit and then took a few steps forward for a running start to make the perfect throw.

"The ball was hit deep, but not real deep, I felt like I had a good shot," Shelby said.

Shelby broke through in 1983, playing 126 games and batting .258 with five homers and 27 RBI. He also had an impressive nine assists in 115 games played in the outfield as teams began to be a bit more hesitant to test his cannon arm. The Orioles often used Shelby as a defensive replacement for longtime center fielder Al Bumbry, especially in the postseason. Bumbry started most of the time—although Shelby got a few starts—but Shelby finished every World Series game for the Orioles.

That platoon system was something the Orioles used to perfection during those years. Using a few players to help out and do one job let different guys get in more games. Shelby, for example, might not have had as much playing time on a team not using that system.

"We won the World Series... so being on the World Series team, anytime you're on that, everyone knows the players," Shelby said. "I think we were probably one of the first teams to be successful using that platoon system. That was something that [manager] Joe Altobelli did [when taking over in 1983]. Earl [Weaver] did it, and Altobelli came in and took over. The team basically took off."

Shelby said it was fun playing on a world championship team as a rookie, because he learned a lot, especially about how things went in a good and settled clubhouse.

"We had good team chemistry, and everyone got along well," Shelby said. "It was just a fun year, especially to be a rookie and win the World Series in your first year in the majors."

He went four for nine in the World Series and got the decisive RBI in Game 4. Shelby came in to pinch-hit for starter Storm Davis in the sixth inning. The Orioles already had scored once that inning to tie the game at 3-3 when Shelby came up with the bases loaded and one out. He hit a sacrifice fly to left field that gave the Orioles a 4-3 lead. The Orioles added a run later and then hung on for a 5-4 win that gave them a three games-to-one lead in the Series—and they closed it out the next day.

"I wasn't nervous at all in the World Series," Shelby said. "The most nervous part was playing the [American League Championship Series] against the White Sox. They had a good team, and all of the games we played against them were close games, [except] for one."

Shelby stayed with the Orioles for a little more than three more seasons, getting traded to the Dodgers during the aforementioned 1987 deal. He then had one of his best seasons in 1988 for the surprising world champion Dodgers. Shelby showed little trouble adjusting to National League life with 10 homers, 64 RBI, and a .264 average.

He also played a big role as the Dodgers shocked the New York Mets in the National League Championship Series. Los Angeles pulled out the series in seven games. The Dodgers then stunned the heavily favored Oakland A's in five games in the World Series.

"Everybody had written us off," Shelby said. "We had real good team chemistry, and we did all the little... things. I think that World Series was more memorable than the 1983 World Series."

Shelby enjoys being a coach and still having a part in baseball.

After coaching stints with both the Pirates and Orioles, he subsequently landed with the Brewers in late 2010.

DAVE CRISCIONE

A Few Brief Moments

D ave Criscione was grinding through his eighth minor league season in early July 1977. Playing catcher with the Rochester Red Wings, then the Orioles' Class AAA farm team, the 26-year-old Criscione's main thoughts were on getting ready to become a father for the first time later that month. That, and getting through another long summer without too much of a chance at making the majors.

But that's when everything changed. Criscione got a huge surprise when the Red Wings were in Toledo one night. Rochester manager Ken Boyer pulled him over after the game to say that Orioles catcher Rick Dempsey had broken his hand that day, and the big club was looking hard at calling Criscione up. Later that night, the deal was done, and Criscione had his first trip to the major leagues.

Criscione spent a little over a month with the Orioles, but quickly became a fan favorite. He got several ovations in the first game he started—a few days after the baby was born—going two for three with a key sacrifice bunt. Criscione followed that with a walkoff home run the next night as the Orioles battled New York and Boston for first place in the American League East.

Overall, Criscione went three for nine in seven games, but became one of the stories that many remember from the 1977 season when the Orioles came up just a little short, and New York won the division and later the World Series. The Orioles had a lot of people come through that year, but Criscione was one that many local fans still remember well.

The whole thing still surprises Criscione, who'd been a very good minor league catcher but just wasn't sure if he'd ever get a shot to play in Balti-

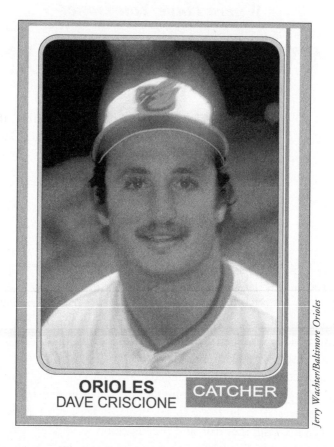

ORIOLES
DAVE CRISCIONE
CATCHER

#40 DAVE CRISCIONE • C
Season with the Orioles: 1977

Best Season with the Orioles: 1977
Highlight Stats from that Season: He had a short stint with the Orioles
that year, his lone stretch in the majors. But Criscione's three hits were
big ones that helped him enjoy life in the majors as he also became a
father and a fan favorite.

more. The funny thing is that everything happened so fast that he literally had to get moving to join the Orioles.

"I was shocked when they called me up," Criscione said. "I left before [getting to pack] my clothes. My wife sent my clothes, which arrived at the same time I did."

Criscione's first appearance came on July 17 in Milwaukee, then competing in the American League. He came in for regular catcher Dave Skaggs. Criscione caught the bottom of the eighth and then got his first at-bat as the Orioles were trying to rally in the top of the ninth. He came up with a runner in scoring position—but lined to second.

The Orioles then broke for the All-Star Game, and Criscione scurried back to Rochester to be with his wife. The baby, a girl named Keri, was born on July 21, and Criscione flew back to Baltimore the next morning and played in the nightcap of a doubleheader with Milwaukee July 24. That's when the fun began.

Criscione was batting eighth and went two for three in the game and had a sacrifice bunt in the eighth that set up the winning run in Baltimore's 4-3 victory as the Orioles were battling for first place. In his first start, Criscione initially came to the plate in the second inning and lined to right. But everything got much better from there.

The rookie then singled to lead off the fourth inning, but was left stranded as the next three batters did nothing. The Orioles had a 2-0 lead. He led off again in the sixth inning and singled again but couldn't score. Milwaukee then scored three runs off starter Rudy May and reliever Dick Drago in the eighth to tie the game, setting up Criscione in the bottom of the inning.

With runners on first and second and none out, Criscione laid down a sacrifice bunt that moved them up. Elliott Maddox later hit a sacrifice fly that gave the Orioles a 4-3 victory. The interesting thing was that the Memorial Stadium crowd gave Criscione a standing ovation after both hits and the sacrifice bunt. The ovations flabbergasted Criscione, especially since this was just his first start.

"Jimmy Frey, who was the first base coach then, told me [at one point] that you've got to tip your hat, kid, or they'll keep doing that," Criscione said with a laugh. "I guess they figured I was just another normal working-class guy who did his job. They understood the game; they knew what I was there to do, and it was a great feeling."

His first major league hit came in that game, the fourth-inning single up the middle off Jerry Augustine. Milwaukee third baseman Sal Bando threw the ball back to the Orioles dugout, and Criscione still has it today. However, things got even better the following night.

Criscione again came in late, after Skaggs was lifted for a pinch hitter. The game was tied at 3-3 in the 11th inning when Criscione came up after Brooks Robinson grounded out. After fouling off a high fastball, Criscione blasted a long shot over the left field fence to give the O's a dramatic 4-3 victory. The crowd went wild again, and Criscione couldn't believe it.

"When I got to second base, I [told myself] to slow down, slow down, it's going to be over before you know it," Criscione said. "Not in my wildest dreams did I expect to hit a home run. I was just looking for something over the plate."

Interestingly, Criscione heard later that the Orioles had planned to send him back down after that game, but manager Earl Weaver told general manager Hank Peters something to the effect of the following, "You tell him. He just hit a home run that won the ballgame and put us in first place."

Criscione never got another hit with the Orioles—or in the majors—but stayed with the team on a long road trip and went back down around August 10. He didn't return to the majors and retired after one more year in the minors.

After that, he eventually wound up working as a supervisor of quality control at INX, an ink company in Dunkirk, New York. Criscione now has been there for more than 22 years, but kept his hand in baseball for a long time. The former catcher helped coach Fredonia State University (New York) in addition to working, often doing his full-time job from 11 p.m. to 7 a.m., so he could get over and help get the fields ready "to my taste."

He coached at Fredonia State from 1980 to 2002, serving as head coach for the last three years and often working as a co-coach with Dale Till before stepping down to concentrate on his full-time job. Criscione took a lot of pride at how well that college team did when he helped coach it and was glad to be able to influence several young players.

But Criscione still has his memories of his brief stint with the Orioles. Criscione's got a picture that shows him rounding third after the big home run, a tape of the radio broadcast of it, plus a picture of the scoreboard announcement that told Memorial Stadium fans he was a new father.

He also wrote the Orioles a very nice email thanking them after writing an article on him in a game program. In addition, he asked if he could get a new hat, because his old one was fading out. The team was more than happy to help him.

"There was no better place to play than Baltimore," Criscione said.

He coached at Fredonia State for 19 years as an assistant and three years as the head coach. Criscione also found success playing other sports and helped raise money for the Special Olympics. He got inducted into the Chautauqua Sports Hall of Fame in 2010.

Where Have You Gone?

MIKE FLANAGAN

From Cy to GM

S imply put, Mike Flanagan was a part of Orioles history in about as
many ways as a pitcher—or person—can be.

Flanagan first came to the team for a short stint in 1975 and stayed for
the majority of his major league career. He went 141-116 in more than 15
years with the Orioles. He also pitched three more seasons with Toronto
and finished 167-143 overall. Flanagan's best year was his 23-9 season in
1979 when he won the Cy Young Award and helped the Orioles to win the
American League championship and get into the World Series.

He came back to baseball after retiring following the 1993 season, serving as the Orioles pitching coach in 1995. But he went to the TV booth,
working as an analyst on Baltimore's broadcasts for two years before taking
a second stint as a pitching coach in 1998. Flanagan then returned to the
TV booth again. He also helped with offseason and Spring Training until
being named as a club vice president along with Jim Beattie in December
2002.

The Orioles then promoted him to executive vice president for baseball
operations after the 2005 season, where he handled the day-to-day business
for that department and helped make the major decisions. But Flanagan
was a man who had truly been there and seen everything with the Orioles,
going all the way back to being a seventh-round pick in the 1973 draft.

"It helps knowing the history, the background of the organization," Flanagan said. "The personnel, probably from top to bottom, from the ushers
to the parking attendants and everywhere else."

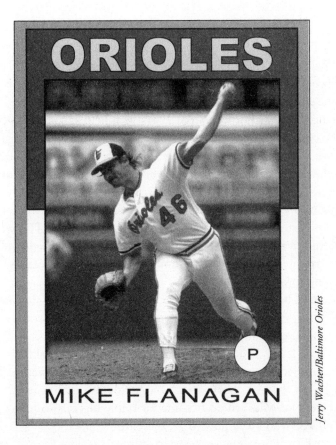

ORIOLES

MIKE FLANAGAN

P

Jerry Wachter/Baltimore Orioles

#46 MIKE FLANAGAN • P
Seasons with the Orioles: 1975-1987, 1991-1992

Best Season with the Orioles: 1979
Highlight Stats from that Season: Flanagan won the Cy Young Award
with a sparkling 23-9 record and a 3.08 ERA. Flanagan also won a game
in both the American League Championship Series and the World Series.

Flanagan worked at turning around a franchise that hadn't had a winning season since 1997 and went through a terrific collapse during the second half of the 2005 season, losing a manager and several players, and going through a bunch of scandals.

At the end of the 2005 season, Flanagan said the Orioles were looking at improving, but may not have needed as much help as some thought.

"The club had a lot of distractions, to say the least," Flanagan said at that time. "We feel good about the depth of the organization going in. When they're ready, they'll come, as opposed to on-the-job training. We want minors to spit out productive players."

What he and Beattie worked at looking for at the time was a solid type of balance that made the team get better. The Orioles of 2005 were a very good hitting team with some good pitching. But they lacked a solid No. 1 starter who could anchor the rotation, and that's what the team was looking for heading into the offseason.

"You need balance," he said. "You look for pitching and defense to carry the load and go with timely hitting, and we've made some strides along that way, and we'll continue to try to improve."

Flanagan faced a lot of pressure as a player when making the major leagues. He had a cup of coffee at the end of the 1975 season. The left-hander began to break through in 1976, going 3-5 in 20 games. Flanagan showed some of what would become his staple in years to follow, being a power pitcher who knew how to get batters out.

But he finally became a solid starter in 1977. The Orioles had made some pitching changes, and the left-hander turned in a strong part of their starting rotation that year, going 15-10 with 15 complete games in his first year as a full-time member of the Orioles starting rotation. That just led to better things, and he won the Cy Young Award after a fine year in 1979. He became the pitcher the Orioles depended upon as they rolled to the American League championship, dominating from start to finish. Flanagan also led the American League in wins that year with the 23 victories.

He went 1-0 in the ALCS against the Angels, winning a wild Game 2. The Orioles took a 9-1 lead at one point before the Angels rallied to slice it to 9-8. The Orioles hung on to win by that score as reliever Don Stanhouse struggled. That was one of the ways Stanhouse earned his nickname "Full Pack." That was how many cigarettes manager Earl Weaver reportedly smoked when the big right-hander pitched.

Flanagan won Game 1 of the World Series against Pittsburgh, again getting a big lead. The Orioles scored five runs in the first inning, but had to hold on for a 5-4 win on a cold October night. It was a wild game where the Orioles knocked out Pittsburgh starter Bruce Kison—who had a crucial role in the Pirates' World Series win over Baltimore eight years earlier—in the first inning, and Flanagan had to strand the tying run on third in the eighth and ninth innings.

He later was involved in one of the more talked-about decisions in that Series. Weaver, whose moves were paying off so handsomely that some media people actually were talking about voting for him as the Series MVP, may have gambled one time too many. With the Orioles up three games to one, Weaver went for the kill, starting Flanagan in Game 5 on just three days' rest.

Flanagan didn't pitch badly at all, giving up just two runs on six hits in six innings, but the Orioles bats fell silent. He left with Baltimore down 2-1, and Pittsburgh went on to win that game 7-1. The Pirates then swept the last two games in Baltimore to pull out the World Series, beating Jim Palmer and Scott McGregor.

Flanagan remained solid in the years after that but never won 20 games again. A knee injury suffered while pitching early in 1983 cost him a big chunk of that year, although he finished with a 12-4 record. He stayed with the Orioles the next few years before Baltimore traded him to Toronto in a pennant race move on August 31, 1987. He stayed with Toronto until being released early in 1990.

The left-hander then came full circle when the Orioles signed him at the age of 39 before the 1991 season. Instead of working as a starter, Flanagan worked out of the bullpen and did a strong job with a 2-7 record and a 2.38 ERA. He also pitched the dramatic final inning of the final game at Memorial Stadium against Detroit. He drew a huge ovation walking in from the bullpen on a cool, sunny Sunday to replace Gregg Olson with one out in the ninth.

Flanagan then struck out the two batters he faced, drawing another large roar from the emotional crowd. The Orioles lost that day 7-1, but nobody really cared.

"Throwing the last pitch of the 1991 season at Memorial Stadium was just great," Flanagan said. "That and starting Game 1 of the 1979 Series were [the two best] moments of my career."

After that, it was time to move upstairs.

Flanagan committed suicide in 2011, something that shook the Oriole organization, affecting many people. It was a subject that, even more than two years later, is hard for many who knew Flanagan to discuss.

JESSE OROSCO

Father Time

J esse Orosco just laughed when asked what he was doing with his life late in 2004. He had retired after setting a major league record with 1,252 appearances in games—all but four in relief.

"Well, I'm not working on my slider now," he said.

Well, he had worked on it long enough. Orosco was the quintessential relief specialist. He was a left-hander with control, the type of pitcher loved by all baseball purists. Orosco served in a number of roles while pitching for eight teams over 24 years. He was a closer in the early days and later moved on to other relief roles, often being the left-hander who came in to face the opposition's tough lefty or only a few batters overall.

He was still trying to figure out where to go and what to do. Orosco was looking for some time to make some decisions.

"I'm just staying home with my kids now, and they're keeping me busy," Orosco said. "I'll take a full year or so off, and then maybe I'll decide which way I'm going to go."

Orosco had told reporters when announcing his retirement at the start of the 2004 season that he didn't feel the fire anymore, something the competitive left-hander always had throughout his career—and a big reason he pitched for so long.

And now it was time to chill out a little.

"I don't want to drift away," he said during a visit to Oriole Park at Camden Yards. "I want to relax, but I'm still following baseball. I feel I deserve my time now."

He had plenty of time in baseball, starting with a long run with the New York Mets. Orosco pitched for 18 games during 1979, making his debut

172

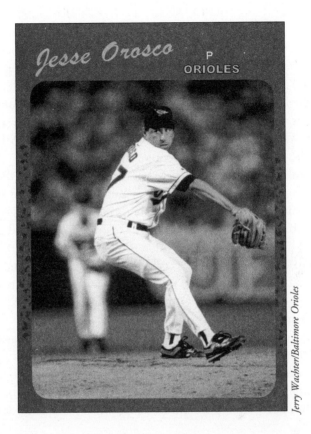

Jerry Wachter/Baltimore Orioles

#47 JESSE OROSCO • P
Seasons with the Orioles: 1995-1999

Best Season with the Orioles: 1997
Highlight Stats from that Season: The lefty played a big role in the Orioles bullpen. He went 6-3 in 71 games with a 2.32 ERA as the Orioles won the American League East. Orosco threw 50⅓ innings in his role as a situational reliever, a role he was very good at that season and throughout his career.

on a bitterly cold April day in Chicago against the Cubs. He also pitched eight games in 1981 before finally getting to the majors for good in 1982.

Orosco became the Mets closer from 1983 to 1987, serving in the role when New York won the World Series in 1986. The left-hander won three games as the Mets captured the wild National League Championship Series in six games. New York won one game in 12 innings and the clincher in 16 innings. Orosco finished both games—coming on in the 14th inning to close out the National League championship.

Orosco also pitched well as New York edged Boston in a thrilling seven-game World Series. He got two saves and appeared in four games. His biggest moments came in Game 7, when the Mets rallied from an early 3-0 deficit to score an 8-5 win and get the team's second world championship.

The left-hander played a key role in that game. He came on in the eighth after Boston had cut the lead to 6-5—and had runners on second and third with no outs. But Orosco coolly retired Rich Gedman, Dave Henderson, and Don Baylor to keep the lead at one. The Mets then scored two insurance runs in the bottom half; Orosco even helped his own cause with an RBI single. He then breezed through the ninth to lock up the title.

"But I was nervous going out in the ninth to get three guys out," Orosco told *Baseball Digest*. "I was pumped up about getting a hit, but I said to myself, 'Don't be thinking about hitting right now. You still got three guys to get out.'"

He did just that, and Orosco later came to Baltimore for the 1995 season after stints with the Dodgers, Brewers, and Indians. He moved nicely into his role as a left-handed reliever who sometimes did other tasks like setup and the occasional save situation. Orosco played a key role in helping the Orioles make the playoffs in 1996 as the wild card team and then winning the American League East championship the next season.

He was the perfect fit for a deep bullpen that carried the Orioles, especially in the 1997 season when Baltimore led from wire to wire in winning its first American League East championship in 14 years. Orosco finished with a 6-3 record despite pitching just 50⅓ innings, but was solid all the way through the season.

Orosco continued to remain solid throughout the rest of his career, staying with the Orioles through 1999 before making stops in St. Louis, Los Angeles, San Diego, New York (Yankees), and Minnesota. His final numbers were impressive, 87-80 in the 1,252 games, and he was always a very dependable pitcher.

Jesse Orosco and Tippy Martinez

"It comes down to you have to still do your job," Orosco said. "It was peaks and valleys. Being healthy and the manager knowing I was going to be out in the bullpen every single day was a big part of my career."

Orosco said playing in Baltimore was a joy. He loved everything about it, especially because the Orioles were in the process of being one of the American League's better teams.

"It was one of the finest cities to play baseball in," Orosco said. "The fans are fantastic, the organization treated me well. I think this is probably the most beautiful stadium (Oriole Park at Camden Yards) in baseball and will be for years to come. I'm surprised that every ballpark doesn't copy them."

He also had a lot of fun in Baltimore that had nothing to do with winning. The left-hander saw Cal Ripken Jr. break Lou Gehrig's record and Orosco set the record for pitching in the most games while at Baltimore.

"I had a lot of good memories here," he said.

Now he's just deciding what kind of new memories to make.

Orosco took it easy for awhile after his retirement. A San Diego baseball business called "Frozen Ropes" announced in late 2012 that Orosco had joined their crew as an instructor and works with his son, Jesse, Jr., who played minor league baseball for a few seasons.

Where Have You Gone?

JACK FISHER

The Kiddie Korps Alumnus

Jack Fisher is taking it easy now. He has been busy and has worked very hard for a long time. The 67-year-old now has retired and is enjoying life at a slower pace. But when one brings up the subject of the famed Kiddie Korps and the Orioles of the early 1960s, Fisher finds plenty of energy.

"When you're young and dumb, you think you can do anything," Fisher said with a laugh. "But we were confident. You get the guys to catch the ball behind you and score a few runs. We all thought we could get people out."

And they often did that. Fisher played a big role in Baltimore's surprise team of the 1960 season. The pitchers were so young that season that they were nicknamed "The Kiddie Korps"—as five starters were 22 or younger—and Fisher was strong throughout the year. The 21-year-old Fisher went 12-11 that year as the Orioles pestered the powerful New York Yankees until the season's final days and eventually finished second in the American League. (There were no divisions back then.)

He eventually pitched in the major leagues for parts of 11 seasons, staying with the Orioles for the first four. Fisher then pitched for some of the downtrodden New York Mets teams that made losing an art form. He also pitched for the Giants, White Sox, and Reds, and finished with an 86-139 career record.

But Fisher eventually moved out of sports after his career ended following the 1969 season. He was a pitching coach for a short while before going to work with a printing company. After that, Fisher took business into his own hands.

ORIOLES

JACK
FISHER
P

Mort Tadder/Baltimore Orioles

#48 JACK FISHER • P
Seasons with the Orioles: 1959-1962

Best Season with the Orioles: 1960
Highlight Stats from that Season: Fisher was a big part of the young
Orioles staff that made them the surprise team of the American League in
1960. He finished 12-11 while making 20 starts and
also throwing in relief 20 times.

He then opened Fat Jack's, a restaurant in Easton, Pennsylvania. The name *Fat Jack's* came from a joking nickname that former Orioles knuckleballer Hoyt Wilhelm gave the six-foot-two, 215-pound pitcher when both were in Baltimore. Fisher worked in the restaurant—and said he enjoyed it a lot—before selling it.

That's why he's taking it easy now, relaxing and having fun. Fisher said he really enjoyed the restaurant but now will try to enjoy retirement. However, something he certainly enjoyed was pitching for the Orioles from 1959 through 1962.

The Kiddie Korps caught the attention of many in baseball and was a huge reason that the Orioles finally broke out after being a losing team for their first several years. The Kiddie Korps featured Fisher, Chuck Estrada (22, 18-11), Milt Pappas (21, 15-11), Steve Barber (22, 10-7), and Jerry Walker (21, 3-4). They were the team's starters for much of the season. Most were workhorses who loved to pile up as many innings as possible— and usually did in an era where starters usually weren't limited to six innings or a certain amount of pitches.

Fisher was one of the pitchers who wanted to throw as much as he could. All five members of the Kiddie Korps had successful major league careers, but Fisher found two of his most famous moments actually came from giving up homers. He surrendered Ted Williams's final career home run in the last week of the 1960 season. Roger Maris then hit his record-tying 60th home run off Fisher late in 1961.

Williams had announced that he would retire following the 1960 season, and Boston's September 28 game with the Orioles would be his last one. Barber started that game and ran into immediate trouble, forcing Fisher to come on in long relief in the bottom of the first. Boston had a 2-0 lead with the bases loaded and none out. Fisher got out of the inning unscathed, and the Orioles rallied to take a 4-2 lead.

But Williams came up in the bottom of the seventh. Fisher felt comfortable, though, having retired him 11 straight times. Williams was only one for 12 in his career against Fisher at that point.

"I really felt that I could throw the ball by him," Fisher said. "The wind was actually blowing in from right field, and I really didn't know that he could get enough on it to clear the fences."

Fisher got to a 1-1 count before Williams crushed a fastball deep to center field for a solo homer, sending the Fenway Park crowd into hysterics and cutting the lead to 4-3. Fisher knew this would be Williams's final game at Fenway Park—what no one knew was that this would be his final game anywhere because the Red Sox didn't announce that until after the game even though they still had one series left—so he stood back off the mound and waited for Williams to take a curtain call that the crowd was demanding.

But the moody Williams didn't come out, and Fisher eventually looked into the Boston dugout. The future Hall of Famer waved at Fisher to pitch—and he never took the curtain call.

"There was a certain aura about him," Fisher said. "He could get your attention when he was kneeling in the on-deck circle. He was just a great hitter. I just went after him, [because] the game situation called for it."

Boston rallied to win 5-4, thanks to a two-run Orioles throwing error in the bottom of the ninth. Fisher took the loss despite pitching almost nine innings of relief.

He wound up involved in another famous home-run situation one year later involving Maris. The Yankees outfielder had spent the summer chasing Babe Ruth's record of 60 homers in a season. The tension clearly affected Maris during the final weeks, but he slowly closed in on the mark.

Maris hadn't homered in three games when the Yankees hosted the Orioles on September 26, 1961. Fisher started and had a 3-1 lead when he decided to throw a curve. It turned out to be a bad choice in that situation.

"I had great luck against him before," Fisher said. "I took a little off, and it just floated up there and hung up there for him."

Maris blasted it toward the short porch then in right field at Yankee Stadium. The ball sailed far over the short porch in right and banged off the railing between the first and second decks. That home run made history briefly until Maris set the new record with his 61st homer on the final day of the 1961 season, a mark that would stand for a long time.

Fisher also wound up losing that game in tough fashion as Baltimore outfielder Jackie Brandt couldn't quite come up with a shoestring catch in the ninth, letting New York rally for a 4-3 win. But Fisher doesn't regret challenging Maris or Williams in those two situations. He said he wanted to go after both of them.

Fisher was traded to the San Francisco Giants after struggling in 1962—his ERA went up to 5.09—in a six-player deal. He later pitched on some of the abysmal Mets team, losing 73 games in four years despite not pitching that badly. Fisher threw the first ball in Shea Stadium in 1964 when pitching for the Mets, who picked him up from the Giants in a special draft after the 1963 season.

Fisher retired from the working world and lives in Easton, Pa.

Where Have You Gone?

DAVEY JOHNSON

The Orioles did not have a winning record from 1998 through 2011. They made the playoffs in both 1996 and 1997 under former Oriole second baseman Davey Johnson, but Johnson resigned when he got the award as Manager of the Year in 1997, and the Orioles seemed to go on a downward spiral after that.

Johnson and owner Peter Angelos apparently argued about different things, which isn't unusual for managers and those above them. But it was easy to see how much Johnson loved coming back to the city where he began his playing career and won two World Series titles. In fact, his remarks from the press conference on 1997 the day he got the award—and resigned—certainly show that.

"You know, coming back to Baltimore—that is where I started; that's where I broke in. I learned to play baseball there, and I came up through the ranks and, you know, was in four World Series and we won two of them," he said, according to a transcript from that press conference. "I got traded away and played in the National League awhile and then managed in the National League. I got the opportunity to come back here, and I'll be forever in debt to Mr. Angelos for that opportunity because he brought me back. I thought we had a great year last year, and he wasn't too happy with it. At the end of this year, there were some problems. I'm sorry they didn't work out, but I will always be in debt to Mr. Angelos for giving me the opportunity to come back to Baltimore."

The Orioles didn't make the playoffs again until 2012. Johnson later went on to manage the Dodgers for two years (1999, 2000) before taking

AP Images/Mark Duncan

#15 DAVEY JOHNSON • 2B
1965-1972

Best Season with the Orioles: 1971
Highlight stats from that season: Johnson won his third straight Gold Glove at second base as the Orioles earned a third consecutive American League pennant. He hit a career-high .282 and banged out 18 homers, and 72 RBI. Those were his best numbers during the eight seasons Johnson played in Baltimore. He later had a 43-homer, 99-RBI season with the Braves (1973).

over the Washington Nationals midway through 2011, when skipper Jim Riggleman stepped down without warning.

Johnson quickly turned that team around, as they won the National League East in 2012 and made a late-season run at the playoffs in 2013 after a very slow start. But that was his final season, as he had previously announced his intention to step down at the age of 70. Still, it will be interesting to see where the Nationals go without Johnson, who had the kind of quick success there that he did with the Orioles and other teams.

He certainly knew how to make bad teams better pretty quickly, and Orioles fans always wondered what would have happened if Johnson had remained in Baltimore.

JEFF CONINE

Jeff Conine played for the Orioles for parts of six seasons. Conine was with the Birds when they weren't very good (1999-2003 and again in 2006), but he turned out to be a consistent player very popular with the Baltimore fans.

Conine finished with 79 homers and 410 RBI in 751 games. No matter where the Orioles put him in the lineup or on the field, Conine did his job—often quietly.

The Orioles used him all over the place, at first and third base, right and left field, and even as the designated hitter. That was the trademark of his career, as Conine finished with 1,982 hits, 214 homers, and 1,071 RBI, plus a .285 batting average over 2,024 games. He also got picked as the team's Most Valuable Player in 2001.

But Conine's best days in the majors came with the Marlins. He played on both of their World Series title teams (1997, 2003), twice got picked as an All-Star (1994, 1995), and now works with the team. His playing career ended in 2007, and Conine now serves as a special assistant to team president David Samson.

In addition, Conine's been working with the team's television broadcasts. He's on the pre-game and postgame shows and is a color analyst during a few games per season. The 2013 season was his fifth year with the TV crew, according to the team's web site.

Conine also finished the brutal 2008 Ford Ironman World Championship, the first former Major League Baseball player to do that. Plus, he founded the Conine All-Star Classic, which is a golf tournament that raises money for the Joe DiMaggio Children's Hospital in Hollywood, Fla.

AP Images

#19 JEFF CONINE • 1B/OF
1999-2003, 2006

Best Season with the Orioles: 2001
Highlight stats from that season: Conine was one of the top players on a poor Orioles team that season. He finished with a .311 average, 14 homers, and 97 RBI along with a career-best 12 stolen bases. Plus, Conine played four positions as well as DH, giving the Orioles help in several different places.

He also was on the Hall of Fame ballot for the first time in 2012, and even though Conine told the *Miami Herald* that there was "no chance" of his getting in, the former Oriole was delighted simply to be considered.

"Never in my wildest dreams did I ever think I could possibly be on a list of a group of names like that after my baseball career was over," he said in the *Miami Herald* in December, 2012. "Just to be on there once is an honor."

Where Have You Gone?

TIPPY MARTINEZ

Tippy Martinez was one of the greatest relief pitchers in Orioles history. Fans just loved that name since it was much cooler than his real moniker (Felix Anthony), and his aunt reportedly gave it to him. However, he also came up with one of the most memorable moments in the World Series championship season of 1983.

Martinez came on in relief versus Toronto on Aug. 24 in a very odd game. Manager Joe Altobelli had made a number of moves which left the Orioles with players in positions that they were not used to. Lenn Sakata was playing catcher when Martinez came on in the 10th inning, something he'd never done professionally, according to an article in *The Baltimore Sun*.

So Martinez wound up getting outs in an unusual way in that 10th inning. He picked off three Blue Jays from first. They knew Sakata had no experience throwing and wanted to make the game a track meet, but Martinez wouldn't have it. He picked three off, and the Orioles went on to win in the bottom of that inning.

"I would call it the oddest game I ever played in," Martinez said in an article in *The Baltimore Sun* in 2008.

The strangest thing about that game is that Martinez was known more for his nasty curveball that any kind of pick-off move. But that night, the pick-off moved saved him—and the Orioles.

Martinez wound up staying in baseball in different ways after his retirement. For example, he served as a volunteer coach at Towson University in Baltimore in the early '90s, did some TV work on Oriole broadcasts, and

AP Images/John Swart

#23 TIPPY MARTINEZ • LHP
1976-1986

Best Season with the Orioles: 1983
Highlight stats from that season: Martinez helped the Orioles to their
third World Series title with his strong work out of the bullpen. The
left-hander with the wicked curveball finished 9-3 with a 2.35 ERA and
21 saves. He also went 1-0 with a 1.00 ERA in nine postseason games.
Martinez helped in the World Series against the Phillies with two saves as
the Orioles won in five games.

later was a pitching coach for the York Revolution for three years (2007-2009).

His daughter, Courtney, became an outstanding lacrosse player (at Maryland) and later was the head coach at Mount St. Mary's and UMBC.

Where Have You Gone?

CHRIS RAY

The Orioles were hoping they had something special in Chris Ray. At first, it looked like they did. Chris Ray could throw hard and throw strikes, the perfect combination for a closer.

Ray performed well as the closer in 2006 and struggled some in 2007 but was still throwing well before problems with his arm showed up midway through that season. He wound up having Tommy John surgery in August and missed 2008, as expected.

The problem is that Ray never was really the same again after that. He threw the ball hard but had what some characterized as a kind of "violent" arm action in his delivery. Whatever the reason, Ray couldn't find the same effectiveness any more.

"I wasn't the same," Ray said in an article in *The Baltimore Sun* in 2013. "When I came back from the surgery in 2009, it was really rough. Just a terrible year. I'd rear back to throw, and it just wasn't there."

It never really came back. By August, 2011, Ray was done in the majors. However, Ray wound up in a career that had nothing to do with baseball, but one he apparently enjoys.

The *Sun* wrote an article in 2013 about how Ray has started running a craft (beer) brewery in Virginia with his brother, even helping to raise money from some sales to support Operation Homefront, a charity that helps military families.

The brewery has three main flavors – Ray Ray's Pale Ale, Main St. Virginia Ale and Pocahoptas IPA—according to the article, all of which are sold around Richmond.

AP Images/Alex Brandon

#37 CHRIS RAY • RHP
2005-2007, 2009

Best Season with the Orioles: 2006
Highlight stats from that season: He went 4-4 that year with 33 saves and a 2.73 ERA. The right-hander struck out 51 and walked just 27 in 66 innings. Ray really appeared to be taking hold of the closer's job for a long time that season. But his arm injury came midway through the following season, and Ray's career then started to go downhill.

EPILOGUE
Gone, But Not Forgotten

Many players or coaches have put on the Orioles uniform since the club began play in 1954, and those who have passed away may not be here anymore, but certainly are in the memories of the lives they touched.

One of the best-known names is Cal Ripken Sr., who passed away in 1999 and left a lasting effect on the Orioles franchise in many ways—not just because two of his sons turned out to be pretty fair baseball players. More than that, it was because of his teaching.

Ripken worked for many years at the minor league level and played a large role in helping teach and coach the players who made up many of the strong Orioles teams of the late 1960s through mid-1980s that were feared by many. Players from that era will often say how much they owe the senior Ripken for his teachings and attitudes.

The teachings in minor league ballparks don't often show up on television or in books, but Ripken's strong work helped lay the foundation for some of the franchise's greatest successes.

Dave McNally was one of the best pitchers in baseball during his time with the Orioles. He came to the team as a free agent in 1960 and quickly made his way to the majors, pitching on Baltimore's four World Series teams in 1966, 1969, 1970, and 1971. McNally was a cunning left-hander, who knew how to mix pitches and rarely got himself in trouble.

McNally played a big role in each of the four World Series the Orioles were in. His unusual bout of wildness in Game 1 of the 1966 Series in Los Angeles let Moe Drabowsky come on in the third inning, finish the game, and help the Orioles to a 5-2 win. But McNally made up for that in a big way a few days later by going in the distance in the Series-clinching win in Game 4, a 1-0 shutout.

McNally also became part of the one of the most famous pictures in Orioles history at the end of that game. When center fielder Paul Blair caught the final out, Brooks Robinson literally took a flying leap toward McNally with catcher Andy Etchebarren right behind him. That picture now is on glass in the second floor of the warehouse at Oriole Park at Camden Yards. He wasn't a fabulous hitter, but showed power on several occasions, the most famous being his grand slam in Game 3 of the 1970 World Series.

He became more famous for something that happened off the field after leaving the Orioles. Baltimore traded him to Montreal after the 1974 season in the Ken Singleton trade, and McNally didn't sign a contract for the next year. He played anyway for part of the season and joined the case with fellow pitcher Andy Messersmith who was testing the reserve clause—and said he was a free agent. An arbitrator agreed and granted him free agency in March 1976.

McNally never played again, but that decision opened the floodgates for free agency and made many players very rich men.